One Square Mile

A Journey of Community Empowerment

D1361801

JOHN C. (JACK) SHAW

COVER CREDITS
Nick Gerda and Voice of OC.org
Michael Connors

ISBN: 1470164469
ISBN 13: 9781470164461

Table of Contents

Preface   vii

Chapter I: From Wintersburg to Oak View—A Story of
    American Migration   1

Chapter II: A Business Model for Community
    Empowerment and Renewal   19

Chapter III: A Focus on the Market and Customers   43

Chapter IV: A Catalyst for Change   51

Chapter V: Implementation—How Do We Get to Our Vision?   67

Chapter VI: Narrowing the Gap—Moving the Needle   79

Chapter VII: The Public Safety and Security Gap—Civic Pride   103

Chapter VIII: The Education Gap—The Ticket to the Future   111

Chapter IX: The Health and Wellness Gap—Why It Matters   125

Chapter X: The Jobs Gap—Economic Freedom   135

Chapter XI: The Housing Gap—Safe, Affordable,
    and Healthy Places to Raise a Family   141

Chapter XII: Economic and Social Enterprise—Building
    a Sustainable Community   151

Chapter XIII: Scaling Up—Exporting the Model   161

Appendix I: Briefing for Congressman Chris Cox, December 4, 2003   169

Appendix II: Strategic Plan, June 2006   173

Dedication

TO PETER F. DRUCKER

1909–2005

MY FRIEND, COLLEAGUE, MENTOR, TEACHER

I once asked Peter how he so often saw the future.
He responded, "I look out the window."

Preface

The One Square Mile Community is Oak View, located in the heart of Huntington Beach, California. This is the story of the empowerment and renewal of Oak View, a story that began nearly fifteen years ago. As I will point out many times during this story, I am chronicling a work in progress. We have not written the end of the story, but we may be at the end of the beginning.

For some of us, the One Square Mile story began in 2003, with a project we called Oak View 2010. The idea that we should be working at a community level versus a program level began to germinate through a series of discussions with community leaders, culminating in a presentation to then-congressman Chris Cox on December 4, 2003. In Appendix I, I am attaching the discussion outline presented to Congressman Cox on that day in order to illustrate that, on the one hand, we were already discussing community renewal, and on the other hand, the fact that we were just "scratching the surface" around the issues of urban hardship. My naiveté is also reflected in that I established a year, 2010, in the title of the project. Little did I know that 2010 would come and go, and we would still be working on issues of empowerment.

This is also a story of self-discovery. I have learned a great deal about myself as I have worked in Oak View and have attempted to convert my business and life lessons to community empowerment. Mostly, I have learned from hundreds of individuals with whom I have worked in Orange County. I will describe my personal journey and those relationships as we precede though this work, but for now, suffice it to say my learning curve has been nearly vertical.

Speaking of a learning curve, this work started out as a how-to book based on my consulting experiences and what I felt it would take to change the condition of Oak View. As I progressed through the thought process of writing the "book," my journey of self-discovery led me to convert it into a journal documenting the trip. Hopefully, there are some lessons that will be helpful to you, the reader, in your own journey of community renewal. I have tried to structure this journal in a way that will help the you to understand the journey and to take action based on my experiences.

Along with many others who will be introduced in this story, the renewal of the Oak View community has been my second career, and my new purpose in life. As a recovering management consultant, I have been trying to put into practice many of the lessons I have learned over a fifty-year career in an effort to demonstrate that these experiences may help renew a community just as they helped many corporations to establish new directions. Of course, what I found out was that some of these experiences were really applicable and worked, while I discovered new experiences along the way. Lifetime learning is alive and well.

This story begins in 1997 with a dream of helping kids who had little chance to graduate from high school to have an opportunity to go to college. My wife, Ellen Shockro, and I were introduced to Oak View as a community by Dr. Bill Vega, then chancellor of the Coast Community College District. Bill recommended the Oak View Elementary School as a place for us to begin to realize our dream. Actually, Bill introduced us to the principal of the Oak View Elementary School, Karen Catabijan, who with her community liaison persons, Fran Andrade and her niece, Sherri Medrano, welcomed us and gave us our start. Little did we realize that nearly fifteen years later, I would have found a second career and would be reporting to work nearly every day at the school, welcomed by the smiling faces of the children, their parents, their teachers, and another great principal, Laura Dale-Pash.

That dream of fifteen years ago became El Viento, an educational program designed not only to help kids and their parents to stay in school and go on to college, but to serve as a starting point for the renewal of the Oak View community. Our One Square Mile community became the focus of all of our efforts to empower the community to renew itself and to take its place among the successful communities of Orange County, California. We set out to demonstrate that community renewal could take place without destroying or gentrifying the community. We became a test case for what is now called "place-based" community development.

We have learned that Oak View, like all communities, is an organization of people, places, institutions, and most importantly, culture. The community is not merely an assemblage of its individual parts, but is really the connections between those parts. Oak View is a mosaic that must be viewed as a whole to be recognized and understood. We really learned that the transformation from urban hardship to community renewal occurs only when the community is viewed in its entirety, where we look for and see the entire picture. Said another way, one cannot simply look at the factors of urban hardship, including

- public safety and security,

- education,

- health and wellness,

- jobs, and

- housing

and address them as individual problems. The transformation from urban hardship to a renewed community happens only when all of the factors are addressed together.

You will undoubtedly notice that I have used many of the examples multiple times during my journey. The examples are repeated mainly because different chapters provide different experiences from the same illustration. One major lesson learned from my journey is that everything is connected so that a particular project, such as the Oak View cleanup, impacts several different aspects of urban hardship and community renewal.

A short walk around the One Square Mile focus of our efforts illustrates the point of the connectedness and the mosaic that is the community. We see young grandmothers holding babies waiting outside the Oak View Elementary School for their charges to be dismissed for the day; day workers standing on the corner of Slater and Koledo waiting to be hired; mothers and fathers working two or three jobs as housekeepers and gardeners; families lined up on Saturday mornings for visits to mobile health clinics; six hundred soccer players and their dads facing off for weekly matches on the school grounds; one hundred men, women, and children wielding brooms for the Saturday cleanup of yards, streets, and alleyways; parents attending leadership and parenting classes; two and three families living in two-bedroom apartments while renting out the corners of the living room at night; graffiti; drugs; gangs; and once a year, high school and college graduation ceremonies.

All these conditions of urban hardship come together to form our community and the starting point for renewal. These conditions also include an underlying culture of strong family values, entrepreneurial spirit, hard work, and a sense of community pride and celebration, without which renewal would not be possible.

Our dream led us to Oak View and El Viento and ultimately to our commitment to helping the community as a whole to become empowered, to change the conditions of urban hardship, and to become renewed. Based on all the experiences of my professional career, I knew we could not enter into the process of renewal by some form of top-down programmatic intervention or by working on the pieces of the mosaic. I knew we could only change the conditions of urban hardship though empowerment and by connecting all the dots between all the pieces of the puzzle. For example, we knew that El Viento was only a piece of the whole community and that even if El Viento succeeded beyond all of our dreams, we would not change the basic condition of the community. Something more had to be done.

To address the issues of urban hardship and renewal, I took a page out of a book I wrote some years ago, *The Service Focus: Developing Winning Game Plans for Service Companies.*[1] The main theme of the work was that of focus on the customer. In support of that theme, the book established the strategies, organizational structures, systems, and processes necessary to understand and serve the needs, wants, and expectations of a specific market segment and its customers. Little did I realize that my journey would reveal that I didn't know what I didn't know.

I saw our One Square Mile community as a market and the residents of that community as the customers for a new breed of service company. We called that company the Oak View Renewal Partnership. The vision, mission, and overarching strategies of the Oak View Renewal Partnership are based on the work I did thirty years ago as I wrote and taught the subject of service sector strategy, so at the beginning we thought we knew what to do. However, this question remained: How do we reverse the conditions of urban hardship and empower the community renew itself? The answer to that question is really the subject of this story.

---

1   Homewood, IL: Dow Jones-Irwin, 1990.

I am extremely grateful to all who have believed in what we are doing with El Viento and the Oak View Renewal Partnership and who have taken the renewal trip with us. I will introduce my fellow travelers as they appear in this story of Oak View, but we would never have gotten started on the trip without the leadership Peter Drucker, my friend, mentor, and colleague of many years. I will refer to Peter many times in this work, as his perspective greatly influenced my view of the world.

Others who helped launch our efforts include Ron Shenkman, chairman of Rainbow Environmental Services, a community based organization that employs many of our residents; Dr. Kenneth Yglesias, retired chancellor of Coast Community College District; Zayda Garcia, chief operations officer of the El Viento Foundation; Armando de la Libertad, former senior vice president of Wells Fargo Bank, now executive director of the Delhi Foundation; Jack Toan, vice president of Wells Fargo Foundation; Roque Barrios, community organizer of Market Creek Plaza; Mike Ruane, executive director of Children and Families Commission of Orange County; and the leaders of Orange County Community Foundation: Judith Swayne, founder; Shelley Hoss, president and CEO; and Todd Hansen, vice president. These leaders helped conceive the trip and establish the pathways to renewal.

Launching an initiative such as the Oak View Renewal Partnership is one thing; funding and providing ongoing support is quite another. We would never have gotten off the ground, much less taken flight, if the following organizations had not had faith in us and believed in the concept of community renewal:

- Wells Fargo Bank and Foundation
- United Way of Orange County
- The California Endowment

- Kaiser Permanente

- Deloitte LLP

Our partners have provided encouragement, financial support, and credibility, without which this journey would not have been taken and this book not written. In particular, Armando de la Libertad and Jack Toan in their roles at Wells Fargo Bank and Foundation; Dr. Juan Carlos Araque, formerly with United Way of Orange County; Greg Hall and Steve Eldred of The California Endowment; and Barbara Shipnuck, formerly with Kaiser Permanente, saw the vision of community empowerment and renewal and provided the resources to launch our new organization.

At this point in my reflections, I must also acknowledge the tremendous support I have received from my firm, Deloitte LLP and Deloitte Consulting. Over the course of the seventeen years since my "retirement," Deloitte has provided significant in-kind support of all the activities outlined in this journal. I have held conferences and board meetings using Deloitte facilities in Costa Mesa and received furniture to outfit the Oak View Renewal Partnership office, as well as computer and graphic support and office space. My colleagues also provided vital management consulting services. A number of my partners have contributed funds in support of El Viento. I have also had the opportunity to work closely with Diana Tracey, my most able administrative assistant. Diana has become a well-known and valuable contributor to all of my efforts. Troy Michaels and his associates in the Technical Services Department have also been a part of my support group.

Our journey is really a journal of our work in progress and is chronicled in the following descriptions of the chapters. The format of each chapter provides a structure for examining the actual Oak View Renewal Partnership experience:

- Introduction
- Structure and Process (alignment and fit with value chain)
- Examples of What Is Working
- Lessons Learned—What I Would Do Differently
- Summary

Chapter I: From Wintersburg to Oak View—A Story of American Migration

Like all communities, the place we call Oak View today has rich history of cultural change and now renewal. An understanding of the community that used to be called Wintersburg is critical to the understanding of Oak View today.

Chapter II: A Business Model for Community Empowerment and Renewal

The books have been written; the bodies of knowledge exist. One need look no further than the works of Peter Drucker on the management of nonprofit organizations, Peter Senge on the subject of systems thinking, and my own work in the areas of the management of service enterprises, to find the frameworks, structures, and strategies for community empowerment and renewal.

Chapter III: A Focus on the Market and Customers

We have created a business model with a focus on the needs, wants, and expectations of our market and its customers. We now must sharpen that focus on the specifics of what needs to be done to serve our market and our customers.

Chapter IV: A Catalyst for Change

As a catalyst for change, the Oak View Renewal Partnership enters into the process for change, facilitates change, but does not become a part of the change that occurs. The community is empowered to discover and lead the way to the change in its condition.

Chapter V: Implementation—How Do We Get to Our Vision?

The Oak View Renewal Partnership, as a catalyst, must empower the community to create a shared vision of the future. The future will not result from a "if we build it, they will come," but rather from purposeful initiatives that will foster the following:

- Leading within the culture of the community

- Achieving a shared vision and mission

- Establishing a set of "first principles" around empowerment

Chapter VI: Narrowing the Gap—Moving the Needle

The Index of Urban Hardship, as established by the Nelson A. Rockefeller Institute of Government, forms the basis for establishing milestones in the journey of renewal and for measuring progress along the way. Further research into the evaluation of "place based" community development activities was conducted for the Oak View Renewal Partnership by the Evaluation Technology Institute (ETI), and is included as an index to this journal.

Chapter VII: The Public Safety and Security Gap—Civic Pride

Communities must first be safe. Communities must also be sources of pride for their residents. Gangs, drugs, graffiti, trash, and health hazards must be replaced by freedom to walk at night and secure places to play.

Chapter VIII: The Education Gap—The Ticket to the Future

Education of all members of the community, from adults to toddlers, is critical to narrowing the gap and creating respected members of the larger system. Knowledge is not only power but also a means of production in our modern economy.

Chapter IX: The Health and Wellness Gap—Why it Matters

Healthy communities are key to education, jobs, and personal success of their members. Prevention, education, and affordable treatment become the keystones of our strategy for economic and social well-being.

Chapter X: The Jobs Gap—Economic Freedom

Our communities may provide the skills and talents necessary to the sustainability of the workforce at large. The need to replace an aging workforce with our younger, entrepreneurial, hardworking residents is imperative to the economic health of our larger communities.

Chapter XI: The Housing Gap—Safe, Affordable, and Healthy Places to Raise a Family

We must work with tenants and property owners to create healthy living spaces without running the risk of gentrification. We seek to create an environment in which our residents wish not to "get out" but to come back and build for the next generation

Chapter XII: Economic and Social Enterprise—Building a Sustainable Community

Establishing economic freedom, creating jobs, and attracting capital are all required to build communities that are self-sustaining, not organizations that are self-perpetuating. A culture of entrepreneurial innovation creates a community with self-sustaining growth and profitability.

Chapter XIII: Scaling Up—Exporting the Model

The current idea of "scaling up" and repeatability is on everyone's agenda. The Oak View Renewal Partnership, "One Square Mile" model, is no exception. We hope that this journal may be the lever to move the concept of renewal to other communities.

John C. (Jack) Shaw
Wintersburg, California

CHAPTER 1

*From Wintersburg To Oakview
—A Story Of American Migration*

---

*Give me your tired, your poor, your huddled masses
yearning to be free.*
**—INSCRIPTION ON THE STATUE OF
LIBERTY**

INTRODUCTION

Ruth and William Slater would not recognize the community often called the "Slater Slum," which despairingly describes its most recent residents. The Slater home on Gothard, which Will Slater built for his bride, Ruth, in 1919, still stand amid what once was a two-hundred-acre ranch growing celery, sugar beets, and lima beans. The house now stands alone amid industrial buildings, warehouses, tire and brake shops, and the One Square Mile community of Oak View. Ruth and Will built their home in a town called Wintersburg, a farming community founded at the turn of the twentieth century by Henry Winters, a pioneer rancher.

Wintersburg, according to Huntington Beach historian Jerry Person, was a self-sustained community within the unincorporated area of Orange County. Wintersburg residents supported their own telephone exchange, post office, and commercial center.

Exhibit I-1, A Wintersburg to Oak View Time Line—1900–2011, depicts the changing demographics and major events that took place over the 110-year period. Wintersburg moved from a 640-acre farming community of two or three families in 1900 to a densely populated center of urban hardship housing upwards of ten thousand individuals living in 20 percent of the original One Square community we now know as Oak View.

Wintersburg to Oak View
Timeline
1900-2011

Wintersburg ≫			≪		**Oak View**			

1900	1910	1940	1970	1980	1990	1995	2000	2010
• Pacific City becomes Huntington Beach	• Slater home built at 17162 Gothard 200+ acres of farm	• Japanese farmers sent to internment camps	• Oak View Elementary School opens	• Oak View Redevelopment Project	• Fran Andrade becomes Oak View community liaison	• Branch library opens	• Oak View Pre-School opens	• Mobile Medical & Dental clinics start
• Wintersburge community Methodist Church opens		1981 Wintersburg Ave becomes Warner Ave	• Oak View Community Center opens	• Oak View Gym opens	• Police sub-station built and "torched"	• New Police sub-station opens	• Oak View Renewal Partnership founded	• HB Mercado opens
• Furuta Family Home		• Bracero Camps	• Oak View Care Center opens		• Lt. Luis Ochoa in charge of community policing	• El Viento founded	• Soccer league starts	• Adult Education school opens at Ocean View High School
			• Oak View Advisory Committee		• Children's Bureau becomes lead agency	• Community Job Center opens	• Community cleanup starts	
					• Oak View task force formed		• Children's Health Initiative comes to Oak View	
							• Community Job Center closes	

Exhibit I-1

In 1904, a small group of Japanese farmers and laborers were also in the process of leaving their mark in Wintersburg. Again, according to Jerry Person, the Japanese arrived to work the celery fields of Wintersburg and in the process founded their own mission on the corner of Wintersburg Avenue (now Warner Avenue) and Nichols. The Furuta family donated an acre of land for the mission chapel that now stands on the corner of Warner and Nichols. The One Square Mile was made up largely of Japanese Farmers until 1941, when many of the residents were detained in the now infamous Internment Camps.

I interviewed Bill Kettler, a gentleman who has lived in Huntington Beach his entire life, eighty-seven years, and is still going strong. Bill has vivid memories of Wintersburg dating back to the 1930s when he attended junior high and high school in the immediate area. Bill knew all of the families who lived in Wintersburg, including the Slaters, Gothards, and Heils, which are now the names of streets that surround the community. Bill's memories also include a devastating earthquake that occurred on March 10, 1933, and a major flood in 1938, during which Wintersburg suffered major damage.

World War II marked the beginning of the downward slide of what is now Oak View. Many of the Japanese farmers lost their properties during their internment and were replaced by Caucasian landowners whose farms were tended by immigrant laborers from Mexico. Nearly three generations later, many of those Mexican workers and their families remain in the One Square Mile community.

As the economics of land ownership changed during the 1950s and 1960s, Wintersburg property became more valuable to real-estate developers, and the farms began to disappear. In 1961, the city of Huntington Beach changed the name of Wintersburg to Oak View. During the sixties and seventies, "White Flight" also took place as the numbers of immigrant laborers began to replace the non-Hispanic residents of the community. Interestingly, during the 1970s, the influx of Vietnamese immigrants represented a significant element of the population. According to Fran Andrade, a second-generation Oak View resident, the population of Oak View included about one-third Mexican-American, one-third Vietnamese-American, and one-third Caucasian residents.

Gary Magill, who from 1975–1979 was a recreation leader for the city of Huntington Beach, also oversaw the Comprehensive Employment Training Act (CETA) until those funds were discontinued. Gary described Oak View as a poor but safe neighborhood until the Vietnamese "Boat People" left to be replaced by immigrant gangs from Mexico. According to Gary, the residents of the Oak View community felt like family, and working with them was "the most rewarding job I ever had."

Martha Werth, who retired from the city of Huntington Beach in 2010, also worked in Oak View from 1977–1980. Martha, on behalf of the Community Services Department, supervised adult education programs and provided organized recreational activities for the children of the community. Like Gary Magill, Martha also reported Oak View to be a stable, but poor community until the "Boat People" left.

Luann Brunsen, who retired in 2010, was very helpful to me in providing much of the primary research into the history of Oak View and the role of the city of Huntington Beach in the development of the community. Luann managed the Federal Housing and Urban Development, Community Development Block Grant (CDBG) funds, including the Community Participation Advisory Board (CPAB) process. It was by means of the CPAB process that the residents were provided with a voice in how such funds were distributed. According to Luann, the development of the Oak View community really began with the United States Housing and Community Development Act of 1974, which provided upwards of $12 million in Federal funds to be directed to such projects as:

- The community center (1976)

- The day care center (1978)

- The Oak View branch library

- The "Tot Lot"

- The skate park

- The police department sub-station

Such improvements in the infrastructure of the community certainly provided a foundation for the social changes that followed.

By the end of the 1980s, the Caucasian and Vietnamese-Americans were gone, leaving a community with no farmland and little hope for the remaining residents, the Mexican-American immigrants and their families.

Until about 1995, Oak View was a very bad place. Lieutenant Gary Faust of Huntington Beach Police Department has a long history of serving the Oak View community. He described Oak View "as one of the most active neighborhoods for drug dealing and using in Orange County." The city of Huntington Beach created dead-end streets and fences to inhibit the movement and escape of drug dealers and their customers. Sneakers hung on utility poles to designate drug-dealing locations. Graffiti was everywhere. Residents would not leave their homes after dark. Gang violence was routine, and murders were not uncommon.

Lieutenant Faust was recruited to serve the Oak View Community in 1995 by Lieutenant Luis Ochoa, a name well-known in Huntington Beach and Orange County law-enforcement and community-development circles. Lieutenant Ochoa, who became a police officer in Huntington Beach in 1965, recalled that Oak View was a Bracero Work Camp. According to Lieutenant Ochoa, the community began its steep downhill slide during the 1970s, driven by the introduction of Mexican gangs and drugs.

Lieutenant Ochoa was put in charge of a police substation located in a trailer that was part of the Oak View Community Center. The trailer had neither restrooms nor air-conditioning. Because the station was located in the center of the community, the residents of the community did not wish to be seen entering the station, resulting in an average of one person per week willing to take the chance. The officers who manned the station did not go outside for fear of their lives, and therefore had no opportunity to establish relationships with the community. The firebombing, which occurred on the second day of the Rodney King riots, April 30, 1992, and shooting of the sub-station changed all that! The station was shut down.

Lieutenant Ochoa, working with the city of Huntington Beach and a local landlord, applied for a Community Development Block Grant to open the current sub-station at the corner of Beach and Slater. The new sub-station became a model of community policing with the hiring of Spanish-speaking officers who got to know the community, its residents, and its culture. The officers of the sub-station clamped down on gangs and drug dealers and built the trust that exists to this day. The visitor rate moved from fifty adult visits per year at the time of the firebombing to over five thousand visits per year at the new location. Lieutenant Ochoa and the city of Huntington Beach led the way to the empowerment and renewal of Oak View, which is now well along in its transition.

STRUCTURE AND PROCESS
The Role of the City of Huntington Beach

Things began to change in 1990s. According to the interviews I conducted as well as personal observations of the past fifteen years, a subtle change in direction began to take place in Oak View. In

1991, Children's Bureau became the lead agency in the Oak View Collaborative, bringing additional resources and partners to the Oak View Community. In about 1995, the focus of the city staff and Oak View partners began to shift from a strategy of containment of the community, and a direct provider of services, to additional partnerships with various agencies to empower its residents.

According to Janeen Laudenback, community services superintendent for the city of Huntington Beach, the city decreased funds available to operate the Oak View Community Center in 2002, resulting in the establishment of an even greater collaboration among other nonprofit organizations providing services to the community. Much to the credit of the public policy of the city, through a new agreement for the operation of the Oak View Family and Community Center, those collaborations were encouraged and fostered. Those organizations, including

- FaCT (Families and Communities Together), through which the Children's Bureau operates the Family Resource Center,
- Oak View Collaborative,
- Collettes,
- Interval House,
- Western Youth Services,
- the Salvation Army,
- Raise Foundation,
- City of Huntington Beach,
- Community Service Programs (CSP),
- El Viento Foundation,

- YMCA,

- Boy Scouts,

- Campfire, USA,

- Girl Scouts,

- Boys and Girls Clubs of Huntington Valley,

- Huntington Beach Central Library, Oak View Branch, and

- Oak View Renewal Partnership,

grew and encouraged active participation by the residents of the community—and empowerment began to take place.

According to Sherri Medrano, community liaison person at the Oak View Elementary School, things at Oak View have improved a lot over the past fifteen years. Sherri, whose family traces its history in the Oak View community back at least three generations, observes that the community is a cleaner, safer, more vibrant place that it was fifteen years ago. Drugs and gangs are nearly all gone; a traffic light has been installed on the corner of Slater and Nichols, the scene of a child's death ten years ago.

The Role of Ocean View School District and Huntington Beach Union High School District

Oak View Elementary School, a Title I school, is also a California Distinguished School. Achieving this recognition is quite an achievement because it means that the school has continued to improve its Academic Performance Index (API) scores, has moved up in its ranking relative to its peer group, and has been continuously been evaluated by the California Department of Education. In fact, Oak View Elementary School moved from an API of 400 in 1999 to nearly 800 in 2011. The school is the "center of gravity" for the community, providing important first steps in the learning process for both students and their parents. Oak View Preschool, under the leadership of Ocean View School District and funded by the Children and Families Commission of Orange County, has become a model for early childhood development and adult education.

Ocean View High School is also a California Distinguished School with over half the enrollment of the school represented by students of the Oak View community. The high school has also taken on the role of community "partner," providing facilities and services that complement those programs offered by other organizations within the community.

The common denominator between the two school districts is public policy directed to community support and leadership. The two schools see the community, its students, and its families as their "customers." The schools are in the "business" of serving those customers. This partnership between the schools and the community will be emphasized in following chapters. The leadership at both the district and school levels is critical to the partnership and to the quality of education provided to the students of the community.

During the mid-1990s, the superintendent of Ocean View School District, Dr. James Tarwater, set the tone for the partnership that was further developed by Dr. Alan Rasmussen and later by Dr. William Loose. The former principal of Oak View Elementary School, Joyce Horowitz, established a culture within the school that has attracted great teachers who love what they do and the children of the community. Laura Dale-Pash is carrying on in Joyce's footsteps.

In 2003, Dr. Van Riley became the superintendent of Huntington Beach Union High School District. Dr. Riley, like Dr. Tarwater, set the tone for community partnership. Dan Bryan became principal of Ocean View High School in 2009. Dan became the mentor of both teachers and students creating a culture of high expectations for learning and a sense of responsibility for the community they serve.

The empowerment and renewal of the Oak View community would not be taking place without the enlightened public policy of the city of Huntington Beach and the leadership of the two school districts.

The Role of the Children and Families Commission of Orange County

In 1998, the Children and Families Commission of Orange County was formed as a result of what is called, "Prop 10," the fifty-cent tax on tobacco products sold in the state of California. The revenues produced by the tax are used specifically to help children age up to age five and their parents to be ready to learn by the time they are ready to enter kindergarten. Mike Ruane, the executive director, whom I will also introduce in the next section, has been instrumental in launching and helping to sustain the Oak View Renewal Partnership. Not only did Mike lead the effort in the development of our first strategic plan, but he also was instrumental in the startup of Healthy Smiles for Kids of Orange County, which will be described in in Chapter IX.

The Children and Families Commission also administers the Orange County AmeriCorps Vista Volunteer program. In that role, the Oak View Renewal Partnership has benefitted enormously by having a series of Vista Volunteers assigned to our organization over the past five years, including:

Britta Strother
Michelle Acosta
Yesenia Navarro
Mollie Grierson
Mike Connors

Our Vistas have done wonderful work in supporting our outreach efforts, managing projects, and helping to run the HB Mercado Certified Farmers Market. I cannot over emphasize the contribution Mike Ruane, his staff, and our Vistas have made to the Oak View Renewal Partnership and the Oak View community.

The Role of the University of California, Irvine

In the spring of 2006, a major lift to the recognition of community-level change was provided by Mike Ruane and the students of the Planning Studio at the University of California, Irvine Department of Policy, Planning, and Design. Mike Ruane, whom I previously introduced, also serving as an adjunct professor at UCI, provided not only guidance to the Oak View Renewal Partnership but also credibility to the entire organization. The strategic plan was developed as a class project with all of the students serving as a consulting team. The strategic plan also provided potential grant makers with something tangible upon which to make their funding decisions.

The strategic plan provided funders with not only a needs assessment but also a sound direction by which the organization could move forward to address those needs. The organizations that provided the initial funds,

- Wells Fargo Foundation,

- United Way of Orange County, and

- Kaiser Permanente,

enabled the Oak View Renewal Partnership to move forward, hire a leader, and proceed to implement the plan. Later on during the implementation of the plan, other organizations provided sustainability to the entire effort, including these:

- The California Endowment

- Hoag Memorial Hospital Presbyterian

- The Samueli Foundation

- The Weingart Foundation

The organization was now in a position to move toward the vision and mission of a new breed of service organization, a corporation dedicated to the renewal of the Oak View community and the empowerment of its residents.

I have included the strategic plan developed by Mike Ruane and his students as an appendix to this journal in the hopes that you will have a greater appreciation of where we started, the recommendations of the study, and where we are today. Indeed, over the past six years, we have implemented a significant number of the strategies outlined in the plan.

The Community as a System

A key element in the strategy of the Oak View Renewal Partnership was the development of a marketing package to be shared with prospective donors and other stakeholders. A white paper was written and a video produced that described the emerging systems approach to community renewal. I partnered with two other community leaders to produce the document: Joseph Ames, a communications consultant, and Dr. Juan Carlos Araque, a leader in the development of public policy efforts on behalf of children. The video was produced by Andy Shomph, a video production consultant, and Terry Ribb, a writer and marketing consultant.

In many respects, the white paper was a precursor to this work in that the authors had to think through the logic of the case and the need to communicate that logic to a variety of audiences. The white paper also served as a basis for research into the broad subject of community renewal.

A Study of Community Renewal

Terry Ribb, who helped produced our video, also undertook a research project to identify characteristics that were common to communities around the world that had experienced successful renewal. As Terry scanned the literature and compared and contrasted communities of differing cultures that had transformed themselves, she identified the following characteristics:

- Collaboration

- Choice

- Creativity

- Commerce

The four Cs, as they have become known, have been used to form the high-level empowerment and renewal strategies of the Oak View Renewal Partnership. Those characteristics form the basis for every initiative undertaken and are the test used to determine how well the initiatives are working.

Future-Focused Activities

As we looked at the various roles of our partners in the creation of value, it became apparent that the following activities required additional support:

- Health and wellness

- Job creation

- Housing

The above activities would form the basis of our strategy for narrowing the gaps between Oak View and the remainder of Orange County.

EXAMPLES OF WHAT IS WORKING

Since 1995, there have been literally scores of examples that illustrate the empowerment and renewal of the Oak View community, examples of individuals coming forward to take the initiative to do what needed to be done to improve their own condition and that of their families, including the following:

- A youth soccer league founded by Jose Luis Rodriquez now consists of over six hundred players and thirty teams.

- Monthly community cleanup, initiated by Zayda Garcia and later led by Martha Jimenez and Ruth Dominguez, is now managed by a collaboration of community partners who turn out nearly one hundred residents one Saturday every month.

- Social-enterprise projects include Emoción, a promotions-products business, and HB Mercado Certified Farmers Market.

- A mobile health program is sponsored by Hoag Memorial Hospital Presbyterian and staffed by Healthy Smiles for Kids of Orange County and the Hurt Mobile Clinic of the Orange County Rescue Mission.

- The Oak View branch of the Huntington Beach Central Library now provides Internet access, reading programs, chess tournaments, and many more activities.

- Community Service Program, Inc., (CSP), provides gang prevention and youth counseling. Under the direction of Elsa Greenfield, and with the support of Carlos De Santiago, CSP works out of the same building on the Oak View Elementary School campus, which houses OVRP. Elsa and her colleagues provide on-site counseling, leadership workshops, enrichment and recreational activities, and many other services for our youth.

- Family Resource Center under the management of the Children's Bureau and with the leadership of Norma Lopez, a member of our advisory board, provides social services on behalf of the County, including family advocacy services, insurance application processing, and many other services.

Many more examples of community partnerships will be outlined in the following chapters.

Getting Started—Rainbow Environmental Services

Rainbow Environmental Services is an important partner in the renewal of the community. Rainbow is an Employee Stock Ownership Program (ESOP) providing meaningful, well-paying jobs for many Oak View residents. Ron Shenkman, chairman of Rainbow and a founding member of the Oak View Renewal Partnership board of directors, is a leading voice on behalf of the community. Ron, a former schoolteacher, city council member, and mayor of Huntington Beach, has provided funding and city-level support for many Oak View programs. When approached with the concept of the Oak View Renewal Partnership, Ron's immediate response was "we have to do this, and we have no choice."

With Ron's sponsorship, the Oak View Renewal Partnership was formally launched in 2005, and a newly published book, *The Tipping Point,* by Malcom Gladwell, was required reading for the board of directors. It was felt that Oak View was at its own "tipping point" and that the Oak View Renewal Partnership was uniquely positioned to dramatically impact the condition of the community.

LESSONS LEARNED—WHAT I WOULD DO DIFFERENTLY

All of the programs that have been introduced into the Oak View community over the past fifteen to twenty years have clearly made a difference in the conditions of the community and its residents. Why is it then that the One Square Mile community ranks so poorly in the index of urban hardship? Why hasn't the "needle on our dashboard" moved and the gap between Oak View and the remainder of Orange County narrowed? What is missing?

The overarching assumption established in the preface to this journal may hold the answer to the rhetorical question "what is missing?" There has been little focus on change at the community level. Most of the initiatives that have been undertaken have been programmatic and focused on individuals and families. While such change is important and has clearly made a difference, the systemic change that produces change at a community level has not been undertaken. Efforts have been undertaken to influence the pieces of the mosaic without considering the whole of the mosaic. Without the organization of the pieces into a coherent whole, the conditions of urban hardship remain.

A conversation I held with a former mayor of Huntington Beach, and the head of a major foundation, is quoted here to illustrate a long-term perspective on community renewal. When I asked for a grant from the foundation, the head of the foundation turned to the former mayor, who responded,

"The City of Huntington Beach spent millions on that community in the 1980s and nothing changed."

To which the head of the foundation replied, *"Then why did you keep spending the money?"*

This was a wake-up call for me. We must prove that renewal can be accomplished at a community level and that our One Square Mile will be worth the investment on the part of the community and its partners. We must move the needle.

The Oak View community and the Oak View Renewal Partnership are clearly works in progress. When the corporation was formed in 2005, the initial name was Oak View 2010, thinking that we would have made substantial, measurable progress by 2010. The name was rejected by the State of California because it included numbers. It is just as well because the name Oak View Renewal Partnership is much more descriptive of the corporate purpose and structure, and the year 2010 was just a milestone in what will become a long journey.

The journey, which began with the founding of El Viento in 1997, has been a long one. Funding a conceptual project such as the Oak View Renewal Partnership has been challenging because the organization does not fall into the programmatic or categorical guidelines of most grant makers. It is difficult to convince a donor organization that all aspects of the community must be worked on simultaneously if change at a community level is to occur.

The story of the empowerment and renewal of the Oak View community will play out over many years, maybe generations. With the benefit of hindsight, and if I knew when we started what I think I know now, I would have done a couple of things differently:

- I would have done much more "grassroots" recruiting. I would have asked more families to become involved and undertake leadership roles and to accept greater responsibility.

- I would seek greater political involvement in the community. The city council is elected at-large with no real community constituency, leaving the residents with little voice. I am acquainted with several members of the council and know that they care about the community. They just don't spend enough time in the community. I must work on that.

SUMMARY

Oak View, née Wintersburg, is a changed place from the community of fifteen years ago. What drove that change? Many factors. First, public policy of containment, shifted from containment to support. Then, as Federal funds began to shrink, public policy again shifted to collaboration among the network of partners that were becoming active in the community. Second, many small initiatives began the process of empowerment and renewal. The community began to take responsibility for its own condition. That is where the community stands today—the end of the beginning.

The changes in the Oak View community did not just start fifteen years ago. Many dedicated people worked very hard during the years leading up to the inflection point at which change became increasingly visible. Those individuals, many of whom I have personally interviewed, dedicated years of their careers to helping the families and children of Oak View to achieve their potential. A common theme among those who worked in Oak View prior to 1995 characterized their efforts and a labor of love. What a wonderful legacy for those who provided the service and those who received those services.

CHAPTER 11

A Business Model For Community Empowerment And Renewal

Today's problems come from yesterday's "solutions."
—PETER SENGE

INTRODUCTION

This is the most formal chapter of my journal. Much of my career was marked by establishing frameworks for analysis, developing processes, and implementing strategy. This chapter is really a summary of what I learned over those fifty years and my efforts to convert those "learnings" to the renewal and empowerment of Oak View. In short, I have documented in this chapter my past journeys in the hope that those trips will be useful to my current challenges. I do believe that my past experiences provide a framework and process for thinking about Oak View.

When viewed from above, the One Square Mile, which is Oak View, is really a mosaic. All of the pieces fit together. A picture emerges. The picture looks like a community. There are streets, houses, stores, alleyways, a school and playground, community gardens, food trucks, offices, Rainbow Environmental Services, and other industrial buildings, vacant lots, and people. There are also walls and fences that define and frame the picture like the borders of a puzzle. The One Square Mile community is an island separated from the rest of Huntington Beach physically, politically, economically, and culturally. It is this island taken as a whole, not in its pieces, that is the focus of the Oak View Renewal Partnership business model.

This chapter discusses and establishes the business model from three perspectives:

1. Establishing a framework for analysis

2. Jack Shaw's answers to Peter Drucker's five questions: "What would Peter say?"

3. The Service Value Chain, how value is created and exchanged

These three perspectives, when taken as a whole, create the structure and framework for a business model, the purpose of which is to empower and renew the Oak View community. This business model, the Oak View Renewal Partnership, is really a pilot organization or proof of concept, established in an effort to demonstrate that the approaches to problem solving and business strategy that work effectively in the for-profit sector will work equally well in the nonprofit sector. In the language of community development professionals, the business model is the theory of change.

STRUCTURE AND PROCESS
Establishing a Framework for Analysis

How we approach or think about a situation or problem often determines whether or not the "right" problem is identified. A framework for analysis is also instrumental in identifying the unintended consequences inherent in any "solution." A long-ago mentor of mine at Deloitte, Don Curtis, often reminded us, "We don't solve problems; we trade the present set of problems for a new set about which we know little."

The Oak View Renewal Partnership business model seeks to renew and empower the community as a whole, but it also takes into consideration the dynamics of how such renewal and empowerment actually take place and produce results. For the purpose of developing a business model that works by addressing the needs of the community as a whole, we contrast two distinctly different frameworks for analysis:

- A traditional, linear approach to problem solving that produces a focus on programs,

- A less conventional, systems approach that focuses on community

This distinction between approaches really matters when it comes to how an organization such as the Oak View Renewal Partnership actually identifies what needs to be done, manages the change process, and evaluates results. The linear approach sees a problem through its pieces, i.e., programs, while the systems approach sees the problem in its entirety, the community, before considering the pieces.

The Linear Approach—A Focus on
Programs, Individuals, and Families

A linear approach to problem solving is commonly used to break down a problem into its parts, establish a "solution," and manage implementation. This approach works quite well with simple, well-defined, and isolated problems. Cause and effect are easily understood, and change is immediate. Exhibit II-1 illustrates a traditional, program approach to the process of addressing the needs of individuals and families within a community. Notice that the approach to the problem is to first deal with the pieces. In the case of social services, this linear model ultimately drives programs, which are introduced as the focus and a means of changing the conditions of the individuals and families.

A Linear Approach to Community Renewal

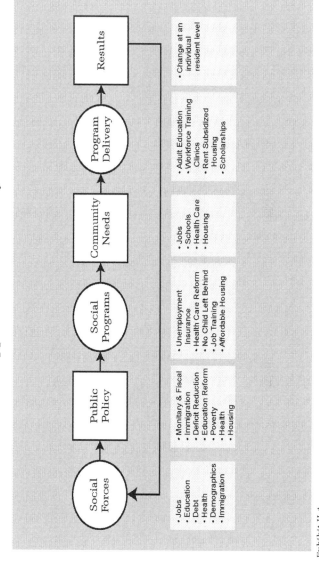

Exhibit II-1

The linear approach to considering social change may be best described by reading Exhibit II-1 from left to right as would normally be the case when reading any Western language. As the mind moves across the page, one step logically leads to another, and in the case of social-services change, from the forces that drive social change to the ultimately recipients of such change, the individuals and their families. Most change is originated by governmental agencies or foundations in the form of programs that move through the levels of government and are managed by departments organized by program. Some, but not many, programs are evaluated at an individual or family level with the results fed back to the sponsoring organizations. Most programs take on a life of their own regardless of effectiveness. The following paragraphs describe the steps though which most programs evolve.

Social forces of poverty, immigration, health, education, jobs, housing, and many others drive public policy. That is, lawmakers and regulators respond to the pressures of their constituents, enacting legislation and accompanying regulations. Most of the legislation and regulation take the form of programs, such as No Child Left Behind, Medicare, Medicaid, food stamps, affordable housing, and others that are managed by federal, state, and local governmental departments. Foundations, corporations, and other organizations also develop social programs under many of the same categories. Governmental agencies and foundations conduct community-needs assessments in an effort to match the needs of the community with the availability of programs that may or may not meet those needs.

The so-called traditional approach clearly channels public and private funds in the form of specific programs designed to address identified needs. The more specific the need and the more directed the program, the greater the impact on the problem to be solved. Health-related issues such as polio and smallpox, which lend themselves to one-time vaccines and immediate results, are very effective using traditional approaches to problem solving. On the other hand, social issues, which are more multi-disciplined, less defined, and less specific as to cause and effect, do not readily lend themselves to traditional approaches to problem solving. Most factors of urban hardship are social, community-based issues, such as culture, language, poverty, education, and so on, which is one of the reasons that the communities of the United States have not become renewed despite all of the programs that have been enacted in the past sixty years.

Affordable-housing programs provide a good example of unintended consequences inherent in a linear approach to thinking about problems. The need for affordable, well-managed, and safe housing is real. The goal of affordable-housing projects is to provide the residents of the community with housing fulfilling those criteria. The problem with the "solution" arises when cities and housing corporations move into a community and rehabilitate those properties. The tenants of those properties are usually evicted. Sometimes alternative housing in the same community is arranged, but most often such housing is not available. As a result, the displaced families move on to other communities, furthering the cycle of urban hardship in another location. In the meantime, the newly rehabilitated properties are rented out to new residents who may or may not have the same cultural histories of the displaced residents. The unintended consequence of such affordable-housing programs is the gentrification of the community. The community looks better and offers new services, but the original problems of overcrowding and the lack of safe, affordable housing have merely moved somewhere else.

The Systems Approach—A Focus on Community

The systems approach is an alternative means of looking at complex problems. The systems approach is very different than the more traditional ways of approaching problems. Inherent in such thinking are concepts such as the following:

- The whole is considered before its parts.

- The parts are not independent of the whole.

- We are all connected in one way or another.

- Cause and effect are related, but not necessarily closely in time.

- There are no problem-free solutions to anything.

The systems approach, often called a holistic framework, is a way of thinking quite foreign to most organizations and individuals because it is not the way we have been taught to solve problems. The systems approach incorporates feedback and learning as integral to the process. Every change provides information. The systems approach forces an organization to consider all of the pieces of the problem somewhat simultaneously and continuously. This is particularly difficult when the mission of an organization is narrowly focused as in a particular program. It is very difficult to see the forest for the trees.

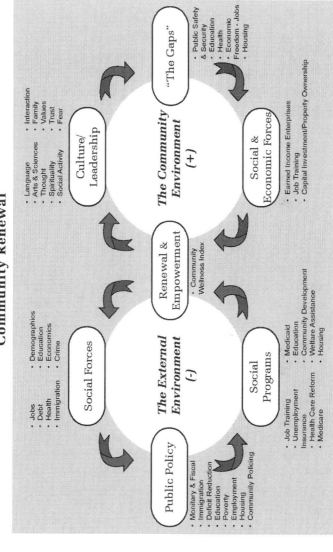

A Systems Approach to Community Renewal

The Community Environment (+)

"The Gaps"
- Public Safety & Security
- Education
- Health
- Economic Freedom - Jobs
- Housing

Culture/Leadership
- Language
- Arts & Sciences
- Thought
- Spirituality
- Social Activity
- Interaction
- Family
- Values
- Trust
- Fear

Social & Economic Forces
- Earned Income Enterprises
- Job Training
- Capital Investment/Property Ownership

Renewal & Empowerment
- Community Wellness Index

The External Environment (-)

Social Forces
- Jobs
- Debt
- Health
- Immigration
- Demographics
- Education
- Economics
- Crime

Public Policy
- Monitary & Fiscal
- Immigration
- Deficit Reduction
- Education
- Poverty
- Employment
- Housing
- Community Policing

Social Programs
- Job Training
- Unemployment Insurance
- Health Care Reform
- Medicare
- Medicaid
- Education
- Community Development
- Welfare Assistance
- Housing

Exhibit II-2

Integral to the concept of the systems approach is a framework called feedback loops. Exhibit II-2 introduces the concept. Such loops are meant to describe relationships in a circular manner, leading to cause and effect, feedback, and learning. We are all linked together in manner that is characterized by the intended and unintended consequences of our actions and relationships with each other. Exhibit II-2 illustrates two very basic feedback loops depicting

- the external environment, those factors over which we have little direct control, and

- the internal environment, our community, which is the focus of our efforts.

Such loops depict, at a very high level, the challenges faced by any organization, including the need to cope with the external environment while at the same time understanding and managing the organization, the internal environment. This understanding includes the need to cope with the outside world of social forces, public policy, and social programs. The forces of the internal environment have to do with culture and leadership, available resources and competencies, capital, and the overall sustainability of the business. It is the interaction and feedback between these forces that determine the success of the enterprise. In the case of the Oak View community, the intersection of the forces of the environment with those of the community will determine the degree to which the vision of the community, empowerment and renewal, will become a reality. In other words, have we moved the needle and narrowed the gap?

Taken together, the intersection of the two loops should provide the basis for a renewed and empowered community. For the community to be thought of as a system, it is critical that the loops be in balance and that they be considered as a whole and not individual parts. This is where the whole becomes greater than the sum of its parts.

Jack Shaw's Answers to Peter Drucker's Five Questions—"What Would Peter Say?"

Peter Drucker, often called "The Father of Modern Management," was known for his penetrating analysis and his ability to look at a problem from perspectives that elude most people. Peter's view of nonprofit organizations and his writings on strategy are highlighted in the following paragraphs

"What would Peter say?" is an often-quoted question that is now addressed when thinking about using a for-profit business model for a nonprofit enterprise dedicated to community renewal. How would Peter answer his five famous questions as those questions relate to our Oak View community and the Oak View Renewal Partnership? Peter's ideas have proved timeless, and although he passed away five years ago, it is fitting that this work be introduced by posing and answering the five questions because those questions form the basis for much of what is being done in establishing the Oak View Renewal Partnership.

What Is My Business?

Peter's first question has to do with the idea of vision—a timeless, over-the-horizon picture of the future. The Oak View Renewal Partnership is in the business of community empowerment and renewal. Establishing a vision or answering the question "what is my business?" is at the heart of the renewal of Oak View. The mindset of those working with the Oak View Renewal Partnership is that of running a business.

The "business" is that of community empowerment and renewal. The changing of the condition of the community from one of urban hardship to one of a vibrant, healthy, successful place to live and work is the business of the Oak View Renewal Partnership.

Iosefa Alofaituli, our executive director, put our vision into operating terms:

> *"A vision of an empowered community forces us to always consider the resident's perspective, which is why OVRP must be on the ground and engaged with community stakeholders."*

Also, as with any business, the organization is responsible for generating revenue, managing costs, and achieving results.

What Is My Mission?

A mission statement deals with the question of how the vision will be realized. The mission of the Oak View Renewal Partnership is to narrow the gap between the Oak View community and the remainder of Orange County, California, along the following dimensions of urban hardship:

- Public safety and security

- Education

- Health

- Economic security—jobs

- Housing

In short, our mission represents the business plan or strategy for renewing the Oak View community. The conditions of urban hardship listed above have been adapted from the work of the Nelson A. Rockefeller Institute of Government. Those conditions represent what the Oak View Renewal Partnership refers to as the Community

Wellness Index (CWI), which will be referred to often in this work. These are the pieces that must be worked on simultaneously to achieve the vision of empowerment and renewal. It is the interconnection of these pieces that represents the "whole," the community.

Who Is My Customer?

This question is one of the most critical and difficult to answer in both for-profit and nonprofit organizations. The answer to this question requires organizational focus. The business of the Oak View Renewal Partnership is focused on the renewal of the Oak View community—One Square Mile—and the empowerment of its residents. In short, the community is the market to be served by the Oak View Renewal Partnership, and the residents are the individual customers.

What Does My Customer Value?

The Oak View Renewal Partnership coordinates, from a variety of sources, a set of value-added services designed to renew the community and empower its residents. The concept of an exchange of value is as important to recognize in the nonprofit sector as it is in the for-profit world. In the for-profit sector, prices and competition to establish value, while the nonprofit sector uses surrogates for value, including "sweat equity," volunteerism, and a desire for self-help to assure that the services being provided really have a value among the recipients of those services. In today's parlance, our customers "have to have some skin in the game."

What Are My Goals?

The Oak View Renewal Partnership seeks to measure results of its impact on the renewal of the community by means of a Community Wellness Index (CWI) designed to track the urban hardship gaps established by our mission statement. The CWI is really a report card to all of our stakeholders that describes how well the business is achieving results.

Peter's questions have been posed and answered. Going forward, the proof of the concept that underlies the business of the Oak View Renewal Partnership will be how well the organization has answered to those questions and whether a for-profit business model will really work to renew and empower the One Square Mile community. Of course, merely answering the questions does not guarantee results. The rigorous implementation of the strategies and operational plans together with accountability for results will renew the Oak View community.

The Service Value Chain

The Service Value Chain is adapted from my earlier work, *The Service Focus: Establishing Winning Game Plans for Service Companies.* The Service Value Chain represents the activities of the business model that, when linked together and actively managed, provide the structure for the creation and exchange of value. Since the Oak View Renewal Partnership is a service enterprise, it seems appropriate here to use a concept that worked very effectively in for-profit service companies. The Service Value Chain is separated into components or activities that are focused on the market and the customer. The activities provide economic value to that particular market and customer, and fit together to form a seamless set of services that meet the needs, wants, and expectations of that market and customer.

The Service Value Chain may also be thought of as the definition of a service itself. In other words, if the purpose of the organization is empowerment and renewal, the activities of the Service Value Chain are the means by which that purpose is achieved. It is the service provided by the Oak View Renewal Partnership.

The Community Renewal Value Chain
Components in the Exchange of Value

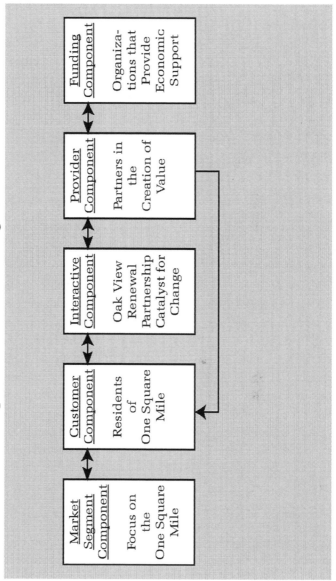

Market Segment Component	Customer Component	Interactive Component	Provider Component	Funding Component
Focus on the One Square Mile	Residents of One Square Mile	Oak View Renewal Partnership Catalyst for Change	Partners in the Creation of Value	Organizations that Provide Economic Support

Exhibit II-3

Exhibit II-3 illustrates the Community Renewal Value Chain for our One Square Mile community—the creation and exchange of value, including the following components:

- The Market Segment Component

- The Customer Component

- The Interactive Component

- The Provider Component

- The Funding Component

The five components must be thought of as an integrated whole, as a set, or more importantly, the parts of a system. While different organizations may perform a particular component or subsystem, all of the components must be aligned and fit together to provide seamless services to the community and its residents. As depicted in Exhibit II-3 above, value flows from right to left though various components to the customer and market. Conversely, the exchange, i.e., "prices" or economic value, flows from the community and its residents to ultimately provide feedback to our funders. Now, let's examine each component in greater depth.

1. The Market Segment Component determines how we establish a focus on the community and its residents. In the case of the Oak View Renewal Partnership, we defined the market segment to be served as our One Square Mile. The demographics and psychographics of our community are well defined and uniform and otherwise meet the test of a served market.

2. The Customer Component consists of the residents of our community, who, when taken as a whole, have a well-defined

and consistent set of needs, wants, and expectations. As we saw in the Community Environment Loop, our community is characterized by a common culture, including language and social interaction. The Oak View Renewal Partnership serves to empower our customers and to enable them to change their own condition. This change in condition of the community and its residents will take place though what we have come to call an exchange of value. The services received by our residents will be earned by means of the residents giving back to the community and to themselves. The gap between the Oak View Community and the remainder of Orange County will be narrowed by the residents, acting as a whole, to change their own condition. We will discuss how this concept actually works in greater depth in Chapter III.

3. The Interactive Component of the Service Value Chain is really the role of the Oak View Renewal Partnership. Our vision, mission, and goals exist to form a catalyst for community change by interacting between the community, its residents, and the providers of the services required to empower the community to change its condition. The Interactive Component serves to integrate the required services to meet the holistic needs of the community as a system. The Interactive Component will provide what we call the Three As:

- Advocacy

- Acquisition of the resources necessary to provide the services

- Accountability and responsibility for results

4. The Provider Component of the Service Value Chain includes those organizations that provide services to the community and its residents. Many, but not all, provider organizations are accessed by the Oak View Renewal Partnership. For the most part, provider organizations secure their own funding to deliver their services to the community; however, in some cases, the Oak View Renewal Partnership may facilitate the acquisition of funds to help the provider organization to fulfill its role in serving the community. There are scores of organizations serving the Oak View community, but for illustrative purposes, the following organizations have been recruited by the Oak View Renewal Partnership:

- Healthy Smiles for Kids of Orange County—a pediatric oral health provider

- The Rescue Mission—a medical and prescription drug provider

- The Grain Project—a partner in providing community gardens

- The Oak View Soccer League—a provider of youth soccer and adult coaching programs

- The Community Cleanup Project—staffed by members of the community and led by our various partners.

5. The Funding Component of the Service Value Chain includes those organizations that fund both the Oak View Renewal Partnership and its provider partners. The Oak View Renewal Partnership, as a catalyst for change, has

accessed resources to fund its own operations as well as selected partners, including the following:

- Wells Fargo Foundation

- United Way of Orange County

- Kaiser Permanente

- The California Endowment

- The Aetna Foundation

- Hoag Memorial Hospital Presbyterian

- The Orange County Community Foundation

- The Pacific Life Foundation

- The Samueli Foundation

- The Weingart Foundation

- Rainbow Environmental Services

- The Thompson Family Foundation

- US Bank

- Union Bank

In addition to those organizations listed above, there are many others that fund Oak View Services. We will discuss some of those organizations in other chapters.

We have now applied a systems approach to thinking about how to tackle the subject of community renewal and empowerment; we have posed and answered Peter Drucker's questions, as well as introduced the concept of an exchange of value through the Service Value Chain. The questions on the table are now these:

- How do we measure change at a community level?

- How do we establish accountability and responsibility for such change?

- Will all that we are trying to do with all of the resources we are applying actually change the condition of the community?

Chapter IV begins the discussion of change management at the community level, while Chapter VI introduces the concepts of evaluation and what has become known as "moving the needle."

EXAMPLES OF WHAT IS WORKING

During the very early days of the Oak View Renewal Partnership, considerable thought went into the needs, wants, and expectations of the residents of the Oak View community. Zayda Garcia, El Viento chief operations officer, and I conducted numerous focus groups and joined community organizations in an effort to engage the leaders of the community. As one might imagine, the same leaders showed up at every venue we attended. Martha Jimenez, a community leader and employee of Oak View Elementary School; Ruth Dominguez, another leader; and Amy Crepeau, family literary specialist at the library, took responsibility for bringing the community together around the early initiatives undertaken by the Oak View Renewal Partnership. Today, Martha is a member of board of directors, and Ruth and Amy are on the advisory board.

Speaking of Martha, I asked her to give me some impressions of her years in the Oak View community. This was her response:

I believe that Martha's observations are shared by most of the residents of our One Square Mile. Martha is unique, however, because she always shows up.

Specifically, the first initiative that was surfaced during the focus groups was the community cleanup day. It was the sense of the group that the community needed to take pride in their surroundings and to take responsibility for the cleanliness of the neighborhood. July 31, 2004, marked the first cleanup day. Nearly eight years later, the cleanup day is still operating during the last Saturday of every month with upward of one hundred residents taking part.

Another major initiative that surfaced as a result of community feedback and empowerment was that of the Oak View soccer league. Jose Luis Rodriquez, now a member of the advisory board, came forward with the idea of starting a soccer league with the fathers as coaches. With contributions

- *All of the programs and agencies are important, but the school is the most important part of Oak View. It is the hook into the community that other programs and services can connect to.*

- *The services available in Oak View have helped the children in my family a lot. The services are there, but some parents don't take the initiative to use them. The parents need to go out and knock on the doors of these programs.*

- *El Viento has been a great help to the parents and families of the community. It has helped keep a lot of our students focused on school and out of the trouble in the streets.*

- *Since I've been here, I have seen so much change in the community because of all of the agencies, including CSP, El Viento, the Library, and the Children's Bureau.*

- *Through the agencies, I have been trained on how to be more active and participate in the community. I learned how I could help others in the community.*

from Rainbow Disposal, Oak View Renewal Partnership, the City of Huntington Beach, and a joint use agreement with the Ocean View School District, the soccer league was started. Today there are more than six hundred children and thirty fathers taking part in events every weekend. The parents and students raised money for uniforms and other equipment. The soccer league has spread far and wide including playing fields furnished buy the Boys and Girls Club of Huntington Valley, and the Ocean View High School.

A large number of examples of community empowerment have surfaced as a result of "listening to the customer" and will be cited as this story of renewal unfolds. In each case, the Oak View Renewal Partnership served as a catalyst and then "got out of the way."

LESSONS LEARNED—WHAT I WOULD DO DIFFERENTLY

As you have probably already discovered, I am a very conceptual person. I have to see the whole before I can visualize its parts. Not everyone sees the world the way I do, and as a result, I have to convert my way of thinking to that of the audience before I am able to properly communicate my message of community empowerment and renewal. I did not do that very well, particularly in the early years, with the result that creating a broad base of support has been very difficult to achieve. I should have started working with an outside marketing consultant who had the capability of converting my conceptual systems approach to something that the intended audience could grasp.

SUMMARY

This is our model for community renewal. We have adapted models designed for other purposes in the for-profit sector to a model for community renewal. We have started to "write the book" at the same time we are undertaking initiatives, some of which are, as yet, unproven. Someone likened what we are trying to do as "changing the engines on an airplane while the plane is in flight."

Yes, the books have been written. What we are trying to do does work in changing the condition of the customer and building organizations that provide focused services to defined markets and customers. When taken together, the answers to Peter Ducker's questions, a systems approach to problem solving, and the service value chain create an organization designed to build on all the work of the past fifteen years to renew and empower our One Square Mile community—Oak View.

CHAPTER III

A Focus On The Market And Customers

The purpose of an organization is to create a customer.
—PETER DRUCKER

INTRODUCTION

The Oak View Renewal Partnership, as a service business, creates value through a focus on the One Square Mile market we call Oak View and its residents we call our customers. A look at the Community Renewal Value Chain of the previous chapter (Exhibit II-3) illustrates what I have come to call the Market Segment and Customer Components of the value chain. A great deal of my work as a management consultant was centered around helping my clients to achieve a *focus* on the market and its customers. Some would say that the most critical activity in the development of strategy is that of defining the characteristics of the market to be served along with the needs, wants, and expectations of the customers that make up each segment.

The business model or theory of change that we are employing in Oak View is that of a new breed of service company—a company created to help empower and renew the community. As I pointed out in Chapter II, this model is unique to the world of community development. I am not a social philosopher or a social economist. I have not focused on the underlying causes of poverty and the tendency of those in poverty to remain in that state. I am a businessman who strongly believes in the forces of the market and in the ideas of individual responsibility and choice. As I stated previously, I believe this model will change the condition of the community and its residents, and as such, may serve as a pilot or model for other community development efforts.

STRUCTURE AND PROCESS
Overarching Strategy
The Oak View Renewal Partnership has a single market to serve—the One Square Mile that comprises the Oak View Community. This market segment is clearly defined in terms of geography, demographics, culture, and need. The Oak View market segment provides a focus for our organization and enables us to directly align and fit the activities in the value chain with the characteristics of the segment. In fact, our mission of narrowing the gaps between the Oak View community and the remainder of Huntington Beach becomes the strategy for serving the market, as we will see in the succeeding chapters. Most importantly, we are not trying to be all things to all people and thereby diffusing our resources.

The market served by the Oak View Renewal Partnership consists of families and individuals who have very similar demographic characteristics, including the following:

- Ninety-seven percent are Hispanic/Latino.

- Ninety percent of the families speak Spanish at home.

- Nearly ten thousand individuals live in 20 percent of our One Square Mile.

Other demographic facts will be presented in the following chapters. For our purposes in establishing a market and customer focus, we recognize that we are serving an extremely poor, isolated community with all of the issues that result from such poverty.

The residents of Oak View, by most measurements, are very poor. Without trying to define what others would call "poor," we can examine the needs, wants, and expectations of those individuals and families that comprise our market.

Needs

The basic survival needs of our customers are being met in one way or another. Everyone has a place to sleep and has enough to eat. The next level of need, those indicators of urban hardship that are clearly not being met, is the work of the Oak View Renewal Partnership. Beyond basic survival needs, there are other needs we are attempting to address, including:

- Freedom from fear

- Self-respect and affiliation

These needs, which are immeasurable with traditional tools, are nevertheless the prerequisites that must be met before the next level of our service delivery process are considered.

Wants

The next level beyond the satisfaction of the basic needs of our customers includes the following:

- Economic security

- Citizenship

- A better life for their children

These wants are within the grasp of our customers, and in many ways, the focus of much of the efforts of the Oak View Renewal Partnership and our community partners.

Expectations

The final level in our hierarchy may be the most difficult of all to achieve. Most of our customers do not have expectations for their future. Understandably, when our families are over-stressed with the day-to-day challenges of life, the ability to stand back and visualize a different condition is nearly impossible. For this reason, the vision of empowerment and renewal is not on the "radar screen" of our customers. Yet without an individual and collective vision of what might be, the community and its residents will be forever stuck in the present. I believe that the concept of a vision shared at the community and customer levels is vital to our work. We will only create an empowered and renewed community if we are able to help our customers to see what is possible.

EXAMPLES OF WHAT IS WORKING
Our Boards

The Oak View Renewal Partnership board of directors and advisory board consist of numerous Oak View residents. Our bimonthly meetings stress the need for empowerment of our residents and renewal of the community. The community leaders who comprise our boards work tirelessly to communicate to their peers the need for their involvement in changing the condition of the community. We have many examples of such involvement, including participation in school activities, serving as volunteers, and taking part in celebrations within the community.

Focus Groups

The ongoing use of focus groups to better understand how we may not only meet our customers' needs and wants but also help them think about their future is an important aspect of our work. We understand that expectations on our part will not automatically translate into a shared vision of the future. We understand that the vision of the future is only truly shared when each member of our community feels the compelling "pull" of a future that is different than the present. Our first focus group conducted seven years ago led to the monthly cleanup, which is ongoing.

Our second focus group, led by Lara Montagne of the Grain Project and Stacey Clinesmith, an independent consultant, determined the feasibility of the development of the HBMercado Certified Farmers Market. Our current focus group is working with our community leaders around the combined subjects of leadership, adult education, and jobs. Future focus groups will continue our work on the future of One Square Mile.

Town Hall Meetings

Using the results of our focus groups, we are in the process of arranging a series of what we are calling town hall meetings to begin the process of helping our customers to see their future and their role in creating that future. We plan to engage a professional facilitator to work with small groups of our customers, perhaps twenty-five to thirty, to begin a dialogue around what it means to have a voice, to have choices, and to take responsibility for the future of their families and the community. We will introduce the concept of exchange of value in terms of what is expected of individuals and their families as they take part in the programs and services that may become available.

Pilot Projects

Among the first of our planned pilot projects is that of adult education coupled with job training. It is our expectation that we will engage ten to fifteen adults to become involved in a job-creation project using the resources and capabilities of our community partners. The pilot job creation project will be designed to fill the first of the "wants" outlined above—economic security. With the placement of our participants in the program, we expect to launch a continuous "pipeline" that will carry more and more of our customers toward the ultimate goal of providing above-minimum-wage jobs.

Exchange of Value

I introduced the concept of exchange of value in Chapter II as an integral element in the Service Value Chain. It has been my experience as well as the experiences of others who serve communities such as Oak View that some exchange between the recipient of a service and the provider of the service must take place in order for the service itself to have value as perceived by the customer. Services that are "free" tend to have little value and are often taken for granted. Said another way, I believe that, in many cases, free services lead down the "slippery slope" of entitlement.

Therefore, as we focus on the market and our customers, we must design services that are valued and for which the customer is willing to pay. As I mentioned in Chapter II, we don't expect to be paid in cash for the services we deliver, but some form of payment such as volunteering, participating in educational programs, and otherwise being involved in the evolution of the community is important.

LESSONS LEARNED—WHAT I WOULD HAVE DONE DIFFERENTLY

Back when we started El Viento, Healthy Smiles for Kids of Orange County, and the Oak View Renewal Partnership, I am not sure that I understood the culture of our community and its customers as well as I do today. In the preface to this journal, I indicated that my learning curve is nearly vertical.

No doubt, I had a lot to learn and still have a lot to learn. For example, I don't think I understood the culture of fear and the consequences of that fear on all that we do. I don't think I fully appreciated how difficult life is for our families. And finally, I am certain that I fully did not understand the "pull" of families on their children to stay close, to work, and otherwise provide support. That is, the family unit as a basic element of the culture drives everything.

Had I understood, at an emotional level, the power of the culture, I would have involved our families in our programs to a greater extent than I did. For example, I would have made our families a greater part of our El Viento and Healthy Smiles programs. Much of the work we are doing with those two programs is making a short-term impact on our children; however, I believe that some of that impact is being undone at home simply because our parents were not made a part of the process of education.

SUMMARY

The Service Value Chain starts with the market and the customer as "drivers" of value throughout the organization. The One Square Mile community represents a well-defined market segment while our customers present a nearly uniform set of needs, wants, and expectations. As with any service organization with the market and customer as a primary focus, strategy, structure, and process will follow. My journey started with Oak View and its residents, and all that we have tried to do over the past fifteen years is to make a difference in both.

CHAPTER IV

A Catalyst For Change

*It is amazing what can be accomplished when you do
not care who gets the credit.*
—HARRY S. TRUMAN

INTRODUCTION

One definition of catalyst is "a person or thing that precipitates an event or change." The Oak View Renewal Partnership, as a catalyst for change, enters into the process but does not become a part of the change that occurs. The Oak View Renewal Partnership is also designed to have a "sunset"; that is, when its mission is accomplished, the organization goes away.

There have been other catalysts in the Oak View community, including the city of Huntington Beach. The city worked to facilitate collaboration among the various organizations serving the community without actually delivering the services. While the city will not go away, so to speak, its influence has greatly diminished over the years as other organizations became more involved. The role of the city, including a reduction in that role, is important to appreciate as a catalyst for change in the community.

As the role of the city was reduced, the Oak View Renewal Partnership came into being to continue that catalytic process. As a catalyst for change, the Oak View Renewal Partnership is designed to temporarily become as one with the community in providing three As:

- Advocacy

- Acquisition of Resources

- Accountability

Advocacy is intended to help the community to find its voice as well as to become the voice for its residents. As the community becomes more empowered to speak for itself on matters of public policy and achieves greater representation in governance, the need for the Oak View Renewal Partnership begins to diminish.

Acquisition of resources facilitates collaboration among the existing organizations within the community as well as procurement of other resources necessary to provide the services required to narrow the gap between Oak View and the remainder of Huntington Beach and Orange County.

Accountability means that the community has to take responsibility for achieving the change to which it is committed. Accountability means achieving the results or outcomes that reflect the changed community. As a catalyst for change, the Oak View Renewal Partnership will help the community to become more accountable.

Finally, lasting change is difficult, messy, and subject to many detours along the way. Lasting change takes a long time. There are no easy or quick fixes. It is only though the continual reinforcement of the vision and mission that the process of change stays on track. The Oak View Renewal Partnership and the families of the Oak View are dedicated to the empowerment of each individual and the renewal of the community.

STRUCTURE AND PROCESS
Overarching Theory of Change

The Oak View Renewal Partnership is a California Not-for-Profit Public Benefit Corporation. The corporation is dedicated to the empowerment and renewal of the Oak View Community, our One Square Mile. The Oak View Renewal Partnership is a service corporation designed to collaborate with its partner organizations to meet the needs, wants, and expectations of the Oak View Community just as any well-organized service organization is focused on its market and customers.

The Oak View Renewal Partnership is not original in its place-based agenda. There are other place-based community service organizations that have been used as reference points for the development of this particular organization, including these:

- Market Creek Plaza in San Diego, California

- Kids Works in Santa Ana, California

- Harlem Children's Zone in New York City

- Dudley Street Neighborhood Initiative in Boston, Massachusetts

- Latino Health Access in Santa Ana, California

- Building Healthy Communities in Santa Ana, California

Each of the above organizations is well funded, well managed, and struggling to achieve results at a community level. To quote *Voices from the Field III*, "There is still no empirical evidence demonstrating that increases in community capacity lead to improved outcomes at the individual, family, or community level, however. Experience to date shows that community-based efforts can partially compensate for, but not solve, the problems of siloed public and private funding."[2]

However, there is one big difference between the initiatives listed above and the Oak View Renewal Partnership in terms of strategy and structure. The Oak View Renewal Partnership, as outlined in Chapter II, is being run like a business. The business model I developed when writing *The Service Focus* provides the strategy and structure for serving a market and its customers. Based on the transfer of knowledge from the private, for-profit sector to the public, nonprofit sector, the Oak View Renewal Partnership represents a different model for community empowerment and renewal. The business model becomes the theory of change.

Critical to the business model or theory of change is the concept of "exchange of value." Exchange of value may become a "first principle" in empowerment. Exchange of value means the customer, or in the case of the Oak View Renewal Partnership, the residents have to have some skin in the game. That is to say, it is not enough to provide "free" services to the community any more than the services provided by any for-profit service organization are free. The exchange of value may take many forms, including becoming a volunteer at the monthly community cleanup, becoming a soccer coach, serving as a teacher aid, attending adult education classes, contributing to a field trip, selling raffle tickets, and serving

---

2   Anne C. Kubisch, Patricia Auspos, Prudence Brown, Tom Dewar (September 9, 2010), Aspen Institute *Voices from the Field III: Lessons and Challenges from Two Decades of Community Change Efforts*.

in community organizations. The watchwords for the Oak View Renewal Partnership become "empowerment versus entitlement."

Following the creation of the Strategic Plan for the Oak View Renewal Partnership by the University of California, Irvine, Department of Public Policy, Planning and Design, and the securing of startup funds, applications for a California Not-for-Profit Public Benefit Corporation and an Internal Revenues Service 501(c)3 tax exemption were made and received. The vision and mission of the Oak View Renewal Partnership became memorialized as a legal entity serving the One Square Mile community.

With funding secured and a legal organization established, day-to-day management was undertaken by Alejandro Tovares, our first executive director. Alejandro began work in the latter part of 2006, and made major contributions to the organization, including the founding of the Oak View Soccer League.

Corporate Governance—Creating the Organization

The Oak View Renewal Partnership was created as a legal organization in 2006 with the conversation of the original advisory board to a fiduciary board of directors. Our original directors included:

- Chairman: Kenneth Yglesias, EdD, chancellor, Coast Community College District

- President & CEO: Jack Shaw, co-founder, El Viento Foundation

- Vice president: Zayda Garcia, chief operations officer, El Viento Foundation

- Secretary/Treasurer: Richard Edmondston, Oak View Property Owners Association

- Ronald Shenkman, chairman, Rainbow Environmental Services

- Marcos Ramirez, program officer, the Fieldstone Foundation

- Martha Jimenez, community leader

- Andy Zimbaldi, president, Alden Management Group

Later on, Paul Castillo of the Waltos Group; Clarence Barker, executive vice president, retired, of the Irvine Company; Scott Smith, formerly of Kaiser Permanente; Joe Ames, a public relations consultant; Vivian Pham of Wells Fargo; Ann Browning, our legal counsel; and Don Thompson, executive director of the Thompson Family Foundation joined the board. At the same time the fiduciary board was being formed, an advisory board was created consisting of those organizations with which the Oak View Renewal Partnership had a collaborative relationship:

- The Orange County Community Housing Corporation

- Ocean View School District, including Oak View Elementary School

- The Oak View branch of the Huntington Beach Library

- The City of Huntington Beach Police Department

- The Boys and Girls Clubs of Huntington Valley

- The Family Resource Center

- Huntington Beach Union High School District, including the Ocean View High School

- The Huntington Beach Community Clinic

- Oak View Soccer League

The combined boards meet frequently to oversee the activities of the corporation and to provide the connectivity between all organizations that serve the Oak View community.

The First Two Years

Creating the organization and getting the funding, while challenging, were not the most difficult aspects of the first two years. The real issues faced by the organization centered around two questions:

- What is the Oak View Renewal Partnership *really*?

- Why is change at a community level necessary?

The vision and mission of the Oak View Renewal Partnership, while sounding grand, offered little in the way of explanation as to what the organization really was and what it was going to do that was not already being done. "Why is such an organization necessary?" was an often-asked question. The obvious reply to the question centered on the history of poverty within the community not withstanding all of the well-meaning work that was being accomplished. One could simply not say to those providing or receiving the services that what was being done was not enough and that real change required a different approach. Those words had little meaning without concrete examples, and there were no examples. It was not enough to say that what was being done was not enough, let's try something different. We had to demonstrate that individual empowerment led to community renewal.

The second question is really an elaboration of the first question. Again, it was not enough to say that a focus on programs does not provide for change in the condition of the community when clearly there had been a change in the community over the past fifteen years. The idea of a gap between the Oak View Community and other surrounding communities had to be established. There had to be a demonstrated need for change, for example, the narrowing of the gap between Oak View and the remainder of Orange County. Again, we needed to prove the "theory of the case," that the narrowing of the urban hardship gap would result from individual empowerment and community renewal.

The "theory of the case," of course, is the application of the principles of systems thinking, the answers to the Peter Drucker questions, and the application of the concepts of the service focus to the One Square Mile community. We had to work on everything at once. We had to prove cause and effect at a community level. This work had never been done!

Therefore, during those first two years, Alejandro Tovares and I spent a great deal of time answering the above questions as well as putting in place our Four Cs:

- Collaboration
- Choice
- Creativity
- Commerce

We collaborated with every organization that would talk to us. We brought to Oak View a Children's Health Initiative, a YMCA fitness program, United Way's Somos Familia Community Learning Project, Orange County Business Council's Latino Education Attainment initiative, and as I mentioned earlier, the Oak View Soccer League.

We put in place plans to provide the residents with choices around healthy eating and exercise, including a farmers market that would not open for nearly four years.

We encouraged creativity in solutions to community problems, including the monthly cleanup and community festivals such as Cinco de Mayo, Mexican Freedom Day, and others.

And, finally, we established a Social Enterprise Venture Fund with the Orange County Community Foundation to fund earned income projects that would benefit the community, including a digital media studio, a promotional products business, as well as the funding for a business plan for the farmers market.

Hitting the Pause Button

As we ended the first two years, toward the end of 2008, our board felt that we needed to hit the pause button on the Oak View Renewal Partnership. We simply did not have the funding or the energy to keep going. We had established ourselves as a credible organization within the community, but our voice was not strong enough to provide sustainability. We shut down the Oak View Renewal Partnership as of December 31, 2008, and returned unused restricted funds to our donors. We had built an organization whose time had not yet come. Alejandro Tovares went on to a very successful position with the Children First Foundation.

During the course of our "pause," I continued to meet with our board and other community leaders and prospective funders. In particular, I was looking for funding and a leader who could provide the energy and enthusiasm to take the Oak View Renewal Partnership to the next level, a sustainable organization. Armando de la Libertad, Jack Toan, and Brenda Gonzales of Wells Fargo Bank and Foundation were instrumental in keeping me focused and involved. They would not let me give up the effort that we had started with so much promise two years earlier. To this day, I am deeply indebted to Armando and my two Wells Fargo colleagues for their persuasive encouragement.

During our hiatus I continued to find, first, the leader, and then the funds to continue. A good friend and colleague, Dottie Andrews, who had been the founding executive director of MOMS

(Maternal Outreach Management System) of Orange County and subsequently interim executive director of Healthy Smiles for Kids of Orange County, brought to my attention a prospective leader. Dottie suggested that I might be interested in meeting Iosefa Alofaituli, a recent Peace Corps graduate. Upon interviewing Iosefa and receiving confirming feedback from selected board members, we had found our person. Wells Fargo supplied the funds to hire Iosefa followed immediately by a grant from The California Endowment. We were ready to take our hand off of the pause button.

The Next Two Years—Hitting the Play Button

Iosefa joined us in May of 2009 and immediately began to establish credibility with the community. We continued to support the soccer league and the monthly cleanup, both of which bring out the very best in our One Square Mile. In addition, Iosefa worked with all of the organizations that support the Oak View community while continuing to communicate our vision and mission. We reinforced the idea of our being a catalyst for change. Iosefa also reinforced the idea that our community partners are the *real* deliverers of services. Our role is to "make the pie bigger" as a result of our role as an advocate for the community.

As we restarted the organization, Paul Castillo agreed to become the chairman of the board. Paul brought a long history of involvement with the community, including working as a counselor with the Community Service Program (CSP). We continued to reinforce our roots within the community.

Our leadership, organizational structure, and strategies were in place. It was time to execute. To once again quote Peter Drucker, "All this planning *should* ultimately degenerate into work."

The Role of Leadership

Nothing happens without leadership!

Dr. Noel Tichey, whose work I have used widely in my consulting practice, in particular *The Leadership Engine*, presents the idea that leaders develop other leaders with what he calls, "a teachable point of view"[3]:

- Ideas

- Values

- E^3—emotion, energy, edge

Clear ideas, strong values, and energy make change happen. The Oak View Renewal Partnership is our teachable model. Everything we do leads to the translation of the for-profit service corporation business model to the nonprofit world. We are learning by doing.

Using our teachable model, our primary task is the creation and sustainability of leadership. Leadership is the scarce resource. We have learned that leadership is scarcer than money.

Of course, along with leadership comes responsibility. We as leaders must be responsible for moving the organization toward our vision and mission. We must be responsible for narrowing the gap. We are responsible to all of our stakeholders in the use of the resources entrusted to us and to achieving the results to which we are all committed.

As we pursue the vision and mission of the Oak View Renewal Partnership, and as we implement our theory of change, we keep reminding ourselves that our business model is not transferrable to other One Square Mile communities without the leadership that makes the model successful.

---

3   *The Leadership Engine*, Harper Business, 1997.

EXAMPLES OF WHAT IS WORKING

Over the course of the next two years, 2009–2011, under Iosefa's leadership, several major initiatives were undertaken to reinforce to catalytic role of the organization. These initiatives would most likely not have occurred without the Oak View Renewal Partnership's commitment to the acquisition of resources. Those initiatives required not only the identification of the services required by the community, but the acquisition of funding, and the measurement of results.

Mobile Health Clinics

In the summer of 2010, Hoag Hospital Presbyterian Foundation agreed to fund a pilot project to bring both a mobile dental clinic and a mobile medical clinic to our community. Healthy Smiles for Kids of Orange County, whose origins began in Oak View, agreed to bring the Smile Mobile to Oak View one Saturday a month to provide oral health education, prevention, and treatment services to the children of the community. The Hurt Clinic of the Orange County Rescue Mission also agreed to bring their mobile clinic to Oak View to complement the services of Healthy Smiles. The two clinics collaborated to bring services to the communities that were not otherwise available.

The access of the dental and medical services to the under-served population of Oak View became important elements in our efforts to narrow the urban hardship gap between Oak View and the remainder of Orange County. The mobile clinics served over two hundred residents during the first year of operation and are well on the way to serving three hundred residents during the second year of operation. Our mobile clinic project is now considered as a permanent program of the Hoag Memorial Hospital Presbyterian Community Medicine Program.

Community Gardens—Community Roots

In December 2010, with funds supplied from the Oak View Renewal Partnership budget, the Grain Project of Santa Ana, working with the students of El Viento and the residents of a property owned by board member Rich Edmondston, built garden boxes to provide fresh vegetables to the residents of their apartment complex. The residents selected the vegetables, were taught how to maintain the garden, and were shown how to prepare healthy meals from the produce of the garden. Plans were immediately made to extend the community gardens project to other apartment complexes in the community including those owned by the Orange County Community Housing Corporation and Jamboree Housing.

There are a number of lessons to be learned from the community gardens project, including the empowerment of the community to become involved and take responsibility for the gardens, the exchange of value between the work required to build and maintain the gardens and the acquisition of the resources to provide the skills, materials, and time to initiate the project, and the role of the Oak View Renewal Partnership to service as a catalyst for the project.

HB Mercado Certified Farmers Market

After four years of planning, the HB Mercado Certified Farmers Market opened for business on May 21, 2011. In many ways, the market is the culmination of all the work that has been put into empowerment and renewal over the past eight years since the idea of the Oak View Renewal Partnership was conceived.

Thanks to the startup funds provided by the Aetna Foundation, Pacific Life Foundation, the Orange County Community Foundation, and Kaiser Permanente, the long-standing project was finally born. The HB Mercado is a great example of collaboration among a large number of organizations in service to the residents of Huntington Beach and the Oak View community.

The market is first a partnership between the Ocean View High School, the permanent site of the weekly event and the Oak View Renewal Partnership. Profits are divided equally among the partners. The management of the market was contracted to Vela, an East Los Angeles organization that operates farmers markets throughout Los Angeles County. Finally, the city of Huntington Beach supported the project from the very beginning, including facilitating all of the licenses, certifications, and permissions necessary to get an endeavor such as this off the ground. The farmers market project, as it is ultimately envisioned, will not only provide convenient shopping for products that meet the needs of the community; it will also provide jobs, community services, healthy foods and lessons in their preparation, and a focal point for the celebration of the culture of the community.

LESSONS LEARNED—WHAT I WOULD DO DIFFERENTLY

The concept of a "catalyst for change" is not intuitively obvious. Organizations tend to first think of themselves and their mission before thinking of collaborating with others. Self-interest is natural. In the case of the Oak View Renewal Partnership, we have an organization whose entire reason for being is that of mustering other resources to work together to serve the community and to make the whole of those resources greater than the sum of its parts. Further, we have built an organization that is designed to go away at some point in time, not to self-perpetuate. When the gap is narrowed and the community is self-sustaining, OVRP goes away.

I could have done a much better job in articulating our vision and mission with our community partners much earlier in the life cycle of OVRP. It is quite possible that the concept of the organization was not as firmly rooted in my own mind as it might have been.

Iosefa Alofaituli came on board and fixed all of that. Iosefa really figured out what I was trying to do. The concept of OVRP is now much clearer to all of us as a result of his hard work.

SUMMARY

How do we empower and renew our One Square Mile without gentrifying the community? How do we keep our culture and sense of community intact while working to narrow the urban hardship gap?

First, of course, is the recognition and risk of the unintended consequences of our actions. Our role as a catalyst is that of becoming a part of the change process without changing the basic formula/DNA of the community—its people and its culture.

Second, all of our initiatives must be thought of as doing *with* the community not *to* the community.

The answer to my two rhetorical questions is, of course, "very carefully."

CHAPTER V

Implementation—How Do We Get To Our Vision?

All this planning should ultimately degenerate into work.

—PETER DRUCKER

INTRODUCTION

During the time I was a student of Peter's, I had the occasion to speak to a group of business leaders with Peter present. I told him that during the course of my remarks I was going to quote him as saying, "All this planning ultimately degenerates into work," whereupon, Peter replied, "That is not what I said." I told him that I had been using that quote for years; what should I have been saying? Peter simply replied, "All this planning *should* ultimately degenerate into work." Another lesson learned.

Implementation and the management of change is really the beginning of the story of empowerment and renewal. Everything flows from how we approach implementation. As a young consultant, I was taught early on that no matter how sophisticated the strategy, if that strategy could not be implemented, it was useless or worse. Don Jennings, one of my first mentors at the firm that was then Touche Ross, was fond of saying, "If the theory won't work in practice, the theory is no good." We were taught as consultants that a deep understanding of the culture of an organization was a prerequisite to any attempts at change. Indeed, if the client did not feel that we understood their organization and its values, change was simply not going to take place, no matter how hard we pushed. In fact, the harder we pushed, the harder the client pushed back.

I feel those same principles apply to community empowerment and renewal. No matter how noble our purpose, if our community and its residents don't think we understand how they live and what they value, they will simply ignore us. As I will point out numerous times in this work, "Change is done *with* people, not *to* people." The operative word is "empathy," putting ourselves in the shoes of others.

STRUCTURE AND PROCESS
Overarching Strategy

Recently, a senior executive of a large, nationally known grant-making organization said to me that "Culture is the eight-hundred-pound gorilla in the room," Of course, she was referring to, in the case of Orange County, California, the Latino/Hispanic culture. The culture is the ultimate determinate of change, yet is does not seem to be politically correct to discuss the role of culture in our attempts to help those in need. Why is that? Are we afraid of being accused of stereotyping, discrimination, targeting, or profiling, or are we simply too uncomfortable discussing the true conditions of poverty in which our communities exist? I believe that it is the latter.

I believe that it is much easier to discuss statistics than the issues involved with twenty adults and children living in a two-bedroom apartment. It is much easier to discuss the abstractions of teenage pregnancy and spousal abuse than the implications on the lives of those involved. It is much easier to discuss the motivation of our customers than it is to discuss the fears our customers live with every day.

I think that if we are really going to use the tools available to us to empower our families and communities, then we must face, in an up-close-and-personal way, the lives of those we seek to empower. Our overarching strategy, therefore, must take into account the culture of the community and the individuals who make up that community. The question, of course, is how.

To help answer my rhetorical question, I asked Iosefa to interview Ruth Dominquez, whom I have previously introduced, on the subject of empowerment and change in the community. Ruth's feelings provide a great example as an example of how the individuals who make up our community articulate the culture, feel about what we are trying to do, and describe their role(s) in the renewal process. Ruth, who is a longtime leader in the community and a member of the OVRP advisory board, is learning to speak English, but for our purposes, Iosefa interviewed her in Spanish and provided a literal translation in the following notes:

Ruth's comments are really important as we think about the culture of our community, how parents feel about their children's education, and how parents feel about their own lives. Without such an understanding, we have little hope establishing a shared vision of empowerment and renewal.

"Drivers" of Change

Implementation, or change management in the case of our One Square Mile community, is all about the motivation of individuals and community to change their own condition *if they so choose.*

- *The reason I originally got active in the community is because when my first child entered kindergarten, I wanted to help him, the teachers, and the school in any way I could. My first involvement with the community came as an aid in the classroom.*

- *My children are my priority, and because I couldn't speak English and support them with their schoolwork at home, I wanted to help out in the classroom.*

- *The motivation for me to do anything in the community comes from my kids. I take responsibility to know and help the neighbors, teachers, and agencies for my kids.*

- *Unlike the past, people in the community know about the cleanup and have become very active. They like the experience of eating donuts, talking to their neighbors, and helping the community.*

- *I've seen a change in people here. They have become much more thankful for the services. One example is that more parents bring gifts to their teachers to show appreciation for the support.*

As a consultant, I was involved in many efforts with what is now called "change management." Early on I learned that, when all is said and done, three factors ultimately determine whether or not an organization and its people are ready for or willing to undertake change

1. Fear

2. Dissatisfaction with the current situation

3. Vision

Fear, while providing a lifesaving shot of adrenalin, is not a sustainable force for change. People are either frozen by fear, or they are forced to take short-term actions that produce difficult, long-term consequences. The culture of our community is embedded with fear—fear of immigration authorities, fear of discrimination, fear of being evicted from their apartments, and fear of being sick without resources. The consequences of such fear include an unwillingness to leave the neighborhood to interact with other communities or service providers, a sense of isolation and powerlessness, and an absence of choices. There are physical walls around Oak View, but those walls are not nearly as high as the walls of fear.

Dissatisfaction with the current situation is a strong motivator for change among most of us. Exceptions to this driver of change include those who come from native environments that they perceive have worse conditions than Oak View. Our residents, for the most part, are not dissatisfied with the conditions in Oak View except for situations that are life threatening. To the best of my knowledge, no one in Oak View has asked to be empowered or expressed the idea of a renewal of their community. Therefore, dissatisfaction with the current situation will not be a motivator for change in the community.

- *People around town know about Oak View and want to come here. They know that there is support from the organizations. It wasn't like that before.*

- *My kids and their education are the top priority. I have to put them ahead of my education and my job. I still attend my classes and work part time, but I know that I have to be here for my kids first.*

- *El Viento has made a huge impact in the community by providing parents with an opportunity to give resources to their kids that wouldn't be possible without El Viento.*

- *When the preschool was built, there was a great positive change in the community. Many of our little children couldn't get educated until kindergarten before the preschool was built. We only had Head Start before that, but they couldn't take all of our children.*

Lastly, the role of vision as a motivator for change may be very powerful in Oak View if such a vision is deeply shared by the community and our customers. The vision of empowerment and renewal must be thought of by our community as having some benefit for its members. Our task is to define that benefit in a way that the vision and its benefits become a force for change.

I have discussed this issue of vision as a motivator for change with a number of people, including Joe Ames, one of our board members. It was Joe's observation that prior to even beginning the dialogue with our residents we must convert the fears our customers experience every day to trust. My response was that in many ways that conversion is underway. It is my belief that community policing has led to a trust of the community in the areas of public safety and security.

Joe Ames put this issue of fear and trust into his own words: "The Oak View Renewal Partnership is working to change the social contract. Where police officers once saw a trouble spot they now see engaged residents, even partners. Where Oak View residents once huddled together, fearful of engaging with the wider community, today they are becoming effective advocates for their community and its aspirations. Once, where distrust, even fear, reigned, trust is blooming."

Further, parents have rightfully placed a great deal of trust in our schools. Where trust does not seem to have been earned is in the areas of health, jobs, and housing. We have a lot of work to do with our service partners to reinforce trust in those areas where trust has been earned and to use those relationships to convert fear into trust in those areas where fear is the greatest. Working in small groups, it is our hope that we may determine the underlying sources of fear, deal with those causes, and work toward a vision of an empowered future.

Assimilation

As I review the literature on immigration and assimilation, I see a mixed message as it relates to those who have migrated from Mexico, documented or not. One message is that second- and third-generation immigrants, over the course of a long period of time, assimilate quite well into the diversified, English-speaking communities. Another message is that many immigrants from Mexico keep their family and cultural ties to Mexico, visit frequently, and intend to return to their native county at some future time. Assimilation and learning to speak English among this latter group is not an issue, and clearly, a vision of empowerment and renewal is not even a consideration. Based on my experience in the Oak View community, assimilation is not a priority. So what do we do to achieve change?

As we consider a shared vision as a "driver" of change, the first question that must be raised is the degree to which our community and its residents *choose* to assimilate their culture into the English-speaking culture of Huntington Beach and the remainder of Orange County. As an "old white guy," this is easy for me to say, and I understand that. What I do believe, after fifteen years of being involved in the community, is that Oak View will always be an island without a voice if that voice is not English.

In subsequent chapters, in particular on the subject of adult education and jobs, I will reinforce the idea that good jobs will require a job-related knowledge of English. Getting a job may well provide the motivation to learn English. Getting a job may be the primary driver of implementation. Our implementation strategy is focusing on the development of leaders and on helping those leaders to become examples of empowerment, which is giving them a voice, hopefully an English voice.

Community Leadership

The basic building blocks of community empowerment and renewal in the Oak View community are centered on the identification, selection, and training of leaders from within the community. This is easy to say and difficult to do. Remember, the Oak View community is made up almost entirely of very poor first- and second-generation immigrants, many from Puebla, Mexico. Individuals with leadership capabilities are difficult to identify. The culture of our residents, among other characteristics, is that of being quite passive and centered around the family and survival. There are not very many adults willing to come forward and volunteer to take a leadership role on any particular initiative.

Over the past fifteen years, we have been able to identify a handful of folks who have overcome their own inhibitions and come forward to work for the betterment of the community. Those leaders are now members of the Oak View Renewal Partnership board of directors and advisory board. Their involvement in our organization is really the first step in providing the community with a voice.

Our job is to provide the leaders who have come forward with the skills they need to identify other potential leaders and to become role models within the community. We are developing a small cadre of individuals who will go out in the community to begin a dialogue around a vision of the future and what that future might mean to the each family. Our task is to empower the community one family at a time.

EXAMPLES OF WHAT IS WORKING

The following, of course, is a work in progress. Many of our efforts are just getting underway; nevertheless, we have come to realize that the keys to empowerment and renewal center on trust, English, and jobs. We discuss, in greater depth, examples of these initiatives in the chapters on education and jobs, but for now it is important to note that a shared vision of empowerment and renewal will not occur without addressing these combined issues. The following projects are key to our implementation strategy.

Trust

Overcoming fear and fostering trust has been underway since the beginning, yet much more work is needed. As I mentioned earlier, we began the process of trust building when the community permitted us to start El Viento fifteen years ago. Without that trust, El Viento would not exist today. It is helpful to use El Viento as an example of trust building and the overcoming of fears on the part of the parents of the El Viento students. My wife, Ellen, and I were completely unknown to Oak View in 1997. We had a dream of sending fourth-graders to college, but that was it. Why should anyone believe us or trust that we would keep our promise to the parents and children?

The trust building began with our meetings with Fran Androtte, the community liaison person at the Oak View Elementary School, and her niece, Sherri Medrano, the current community liaison person. Fran and Sherri listened to what we wanted to do and gave us a chance. Those two women trusted Ellen and me and subsequently transferred their trust to our families and children.

The El Viento parents did not just give us their trust and that was the end of it. Those parents accompanied their children and us on field trips, to their swimming and sailing lessons, and attended parent meetings led by Dr. Kenneth Yglesias, then president of Golden West College, one of our partner organizations.

Over time, the parents overcame their fears of outsiders and came to know that Ellen and I wanted the same things for their children that they wanted. Overcoming fear and transferring that fear to trust was a big part of the ultimate success of El Viento. It is my belief that we must do the same thing with other aspects of our implementation process.

Workforce Development/Jobs Pipeline

Iosefa Alofaituli, our executive director, is putting in place a formal program of community engagement, case management, skills training, workforce development, and job placement. This program, the planning for which got underway in the fall of 2011, brings together our community partners, including:

- Taller San Jose

- Working Wardrobes

- Huntington Beach Adult School

- Goodwill (Employment Works)

- El Viento Foundation

We plan to bring on board a community job developer/case manager whose primary tasks will include the following:

- Engaging the job needs of our residents

- Developing a network of local workforce partners

- Developing a network of prospective local employers/ businesses

- Developing/facilitating workshops

Our community job developer/case manager will collaborate with other community organizations to identify twenty to thirty adult residents to form a pilot group that will be trained in appropriate job skills and English. Our pilot group will ultimately become role models for the remainder of the community and will take the responsibility for engaging more and more members of the community.

El Viento Foundation

Under the leadership of Zayda Garcia, the El Viento chief operations officer, we have had programs in the works for the past fifteen years to educate small groups of students in the community, beginning in the fourth grade and extending through college scholarships. The program, as discussed in other chapters, has had a very positive impact on attitudes toward education, in particular the desire of our parents for a better life for their children.

While we involved the parents in the program since the very beginning, we have not addressed their need for acquiring job skills and English proficiency. We plan to introduce our Work Force Development/Jobs Pipeline project to our El Viento parents in an effort to enable them not only to help their children to achieve a better life, but to help themselves to better lives.

LESSONS LEARNED—WHAT I WOULD HAVE DONE DIFFERENTLY

The quick answer to my question is that I would have started everything sooner. The big *if* is the question of whether or not it would have been possible to start everything sooner. Trust had to be built, and of course, that takes time. Awareness and learning on the part of all of us had to take place, and of course, that has taken time and is continuing. Except for Market Creek Plaza in San Diego, we really didn't have any models to follow. Market Creek Plaza clearly has implemented change though commerce and the creation of jobs for the community.

But, as we saw it at the time, Market Creek Plaza was so capital intensive in terms of commercial-real-estate development that we did not learn the lessons of community empowerment. We knew Roque Barros had spent two years going from door to door understanding the needs of the community, but I don't think I fully appreciated his story. I was looking at the problem from my perspective rather than through Roque's eyes.

The greatest lesson I have learned personally is the well-established notion that "a way of seeing is a way of not seeing." I was seeing the community as I would have it be as opposed to how the community and its customers would have it be.

SUMMARY

Trust, jobs, and English! Creating a shared vision of empowerment and renewal on the part of the community and our customers must occur as a result of self-interest. That self-interest must be fueled though economic incentives—meaningful, well-paying jobs—which is only possible through the development of marketable skills and the language of those skills, English.

CHAPTER VI

Narrowing The Gap—
Moving The Needle

If you can't measure it, you can't manage it.
—PETER DRUCKER

INTRODUCTION

My mentor, Peter Drucker, has been often quoted as saying, "If you can't measure it, you can't manage it." I don't know for certain that Peter actually uttered those words, but I do believe, just as Peter believed, that outcomes and results are important. I think Peter also shared with me the belief that the really important things, such as culture and leadership, can't be measured.

As a business, the Oak View Renewal Partnership is responsible for achieving results, in this case, moving toward our vision of empowerment and renewal. Achieving our mission of narrowing the gap between the Oak View community and the remainder of Orange County will serve as evidence of the results of our empowerment and renewal efforts. The question that needs to be answered, of course, is "how do we know that we are narrowing the gap?"

Systems thinking teaches us that cause and effect are not closely related in time or space. Programs, projects, and initiatives undertaken today will often show results far into the future and in many different forms. Therefore, this question of narrowing the gap is a very difficult one to answer. In fact, we may not know the results of our efforts for many years. Yet not being able to answer the question in the short term is no excuse for our not attempting to put such measurements in place.

Early in the history of the Oak View Renewal Partnership, questions around the measurement of success were frequently discussed. Our advisory board and later our board of directors realized that a new model for community empowerment and renewal would require a "proof of concept." That proof of concept would include a qualitative and quantitative set of metrics that would measure the breadth and depth of our efforts.

A search of the available literature at the time revealed only one comprehensive set of measurements that attempted to portray the social and economic status of a census tract. The Nelson A. Rockefeller Institute of Government produced such studies known as the Intercity Hardship Index. Much of our work over the past five years has used this index as its base.

We have also worked closely with the Center for Demographic Research at California State University, Fullerton, Evaluation & Training Institute (ETI), and the Orange County Health Needs Assessment (OCHNA), in our efforts to establish a baseline for evaluation and to measure changes against that baseline.

We realize that numbers cannot and do not measure everything related to narrowing the gap. While most things that are really important cannot be measured, we at least know where we are on several important dimensions, and we have some idea of what needs to be done to improve the condition of Oak View.

STRUCTURE AND PROCESS
Establishing a Framework for Analysis

As I mentioned above, we started with the Rockefeller Institute Intercity Hardship Index,[4] which measures six key factors:

- Unemployment, defined as the percent of the civilian population over the age of sixteen who are unemployed

- Dependency, the percentage of the population that are under the age of eighteen or over the age of sixty-four

- Education, the percentage of the population over the age of twenty-five who have less than a high-school education

- Income level, the per-capita income

- Crowded housing, measured by the percent of occupied housing units with more than one person per room

- Poverty, the percent of people living below the federal poverty level

For each city, the values on the above six factors are compared to a national standard, and they are given equal weight when combined in a composite index. A higher Intercity Hardship Index score signifies worse economic conditions.

While the above index served as a good starting point, in particular using census data, there were several missing elements, including public safety and security, and health. With the inclusion of these issues, we now felt that we had a proper framework for analysis, one that would provide a reliable base for comparison with other communities.

---

4   Lisa M. Montiel, Richard P. Nathan, and David J Wright (August 2004), "An Update on Urban Hardship," The Nelson A. Rockefeller Institute of Government—Urban and Metropolitan Studies, p.1.

Community Wellness Index (CWI)

In 2008, we combined the Intercity Hardship Index metrics with a survey of the local community to establish what we now call a Community Wellness Index (CWI). See Exhibits VI-1–5 below. The Community Wellness Index was established as an appendix of a monograph, *The Community as a System: The "One Square Mile" Approach in Orange County*. My colleagues, Juan Carlos Araque, Ph.D., and Joseph Ames, collaborated to publish an overall approach to community empowerment and renewal that, in many respects, formed the basis for this work.

The objective of the CWI was to establish a set of metrics that would become reliable, repeatable indicators as to whether or not we were accomplishing our mission of narrowing the gap between Oak View and the remainder of Orange County. In short, are we moving the needle?

As we think about the CWI, it is useful to consider the indicator as a dashboard of our performance. As with the dashboard of an automobile or an airplane, no single indicator ever tells the whole story of the situation faced by the driver or the pilot. The driver or the pilot is always scanning the instrument panel to examine "off-normal" conditions or situations that require further examination. It is a balance of the readings of the indicators that tell the whole story. So it is with the CWI. We are constantly looking at the conditions of the community in an effort to see which combination of efforts seems to be producing the desired outcomes, or which efforts seem to be having little impact.

From a measurement viewpoint, the fact that Oak View is contained within two block groups of a single census tract is very convenient. Our ability to gather reliable, comparative data is made much easier than would be the case if we were required to use zip codes, school district boundaries, or other political zones. The use of census data, including the constant updates available from Federal data bases, including American Fact Finder, the American Community Survey, and the Nielsen Claritas database, greatly simplify the collection, analysis, and presentation of the CWI "report card."

Public safety and security and health are two major exceptions to the CWI that require original research, as neither of those data elements is available through census-related sources. Also, high-school graduation rates have to be separately established for the Oak View community.

Exhibits VI-1–5 have several missing elements. We included our proposed data elements as well as those elements that are known just to indicate that ours is a work in progress, and we fully intend to fill in those blanks and to include other outcomes as we continue our journey.

I converted the CWI from its original table form to graphic bar charts and pie charts in an effort to provide a more visual reference to the gaps we are working to narrow. Exhibits VI-1–5 also illustrate the trend between our 2008 starting points and the 2011 situation.

Taking a closer look at each major indicator, I would like to highlight what we know and don't know about each measurement:

- Exhibit VI-1: Public Safety and Security
  We have more work to do to make our Orange County and Oak View data more comparable, but when Orange County is compared to Orange County and Oak View to Oak View, we see valid comparisons.

- Exhibit VI-2: Education
  As of this moment, we don't have Oak View graduation rates, but given the downward trend of the population without a high-school diploma, I think we will see the graduation rate increase in 2007–2011.

- Exhibit VI-3: Health
  Our fitness and obesity rates have improved from 2007–2011, thanks to the work of all of our partners. There are, of course, many other metrics that depict community health, and we plan to continue to update this gap as more data is gathered.

- Exhibit VI-4: Housing
  It should come as no surprise that our housing data has not changed much between 2007 and 2011.

- Exhibit VI-5: Jobs/Income Security
  While the percent of our population that lives below the poverty line has increased slightly, the per-capita income has increased. We don't have employment data for 2007, but we will continue to track the unemployment and not-in-the-labor-force data very carefully.

Our CWI is clearly a work in progress, and subsequent editions of this journal will include such updates.

There are two other important aspects of the CWI:

- The CWI is not static; it is dynamic. By that I mean we are continuously measuring change in an effort to track our empowerment and renewal efforts.

- Even though it is impossible to directly measure cause and effect, the very fact that we are measuring change on many dimensions provides credibility to our efforts.

Index of Orange County Urban Hardship

In 2009, we began work with the Center for Demographic Research at California State University, Fullerton, (CSUF) in an effort to bring the Intercity Hardship Institute Index and the Community Wellness Index together and to make them comparable to other census tracts in Orange County. We wanted such comparisons, of course, to determine whether or not we were changing the comparative rankings of urban hardship.

Exhibit VI-6 illustrates the relationship between Oak View and other Orange County communities having similar demographic characteristics. The center, led by Debora Diep with her colleagues Scott Smith and Jason Touchette, provided valuable consulting and research assistance as we worked to develop useful ways of assessing and comparing Oak View to other, similar communities in Orange County.

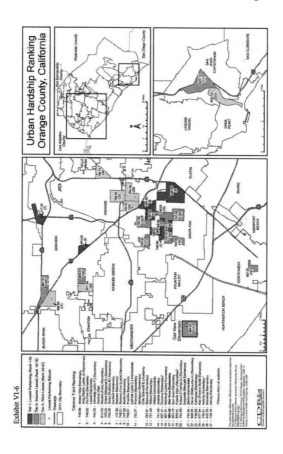

The Oak View community is currently "tied" for seventeenth place among the twenty-seven comparable census tracts illustrated in Exhibit VI-6. Of course, our goal is to "fall out" of the twenty-seven rankings entirely as we move the needle, narrow the gap between Oak View and the remainder of Orange County.

Evaluation & Training Institute (ETI)

Also in 2009, we worked with the Evaluation Technology Institute in Los Angeles to seek their assistance in evaluating various programs undertaken by OVRP as well as to gain their insights into how to measure outcomes for the community as a whole. ETI did a great job of analysis and literature research, but interestingly could not identify any evaluation programs that measured change at a community level. As we experienced in discussions with other organizations, there is no body of knowledge or framework for analysis that attempts to measure change across multiple programs within a community. Analysis at a community level just does not seem to exist.

A Test of the Business Model or Theory of Change

When all is said and done, and to paraphrase Voltaire, we can't let the perfect be the enemy of good. We need measurements that are "good enough" for our purposes without having to take our results out to three decimal places. We need credible, reliable, repeatable data and analysis because we need answers now, not at some time in the future.

Once the framework for analysis was established and a process created for continuing the update and comparison between Oak View and the remainder of Orange County, the next question to be answered was "will the Community Wellness Index measure how well the business model is working?"

We believe that, over time, the answer to this rhetorical question is a resounding YES! On the qualitative side of our evaluations outcomes, we have seen dramatic change in Oak View community since the police department sub-station was firebombed in 1993. Oak View is a safe and secure place to live. On the quantitative side, we believe the "needle" will start to move if for no other reason than we are paying attention to what is important.

In the short term, the needle may not move very much. There are enormous issues confronting Oak View, including the greatest economic downturn since the Great Depression, and perhaps most important, the inertia of culture.

EXAMPLES OF WHAT IS WORKING
Monthly Neighborhood Cleanup

In 2004, as we were conceiving the notion of a community-based organization, then called Oak View 2010, Zayda Garcia and I conducted a series of focus-group meetings with a number of the community leaders. The purpose of those meetings was to listen to our "customers," to identify their needs, wants, and expectations, and to establish a rough set of priorities for possible change initiatives. First on the list of initiatives was the creation of a monthly cleanup project to be staffed by members of the community.

For a whole set of reasons, the alleys and trash bins were overloaded with used furniture, trash, broken equipment, etc. Since the alleys and trash bins were community facilities, not "owned" by a particular family or apartment, there was little incentive to make certain that those facilities were maintained in a safe and healthy manner. The result, at a community level, was a very unsafe, unsightly, and unhealthy condition.

Over the six-year period since the monthly neighborhood cleanup began, the attendance and participation by the community members has moved from a few concerned mothers, Zayda, and me

- *The most important piece of the community is Oak View School. It's the center of the community, the fabric that all of the other agencies stem from.*

- *Alejandro and I trusted each other, and together we started the league. It started with a community forum of two hundred people to talk about building the league. We went from having eleven teams to over thirty teams today. With people like Martin (former FRC director), Sherri, and Iosefa, we have been able to continue to build this league.*

- *What motivated me to develop the league was that I wanted the youth to be able to develop themselves through soccer. I wanted to provide access to soccer that is close to home since many of our people don't have a way to get to Santa Ana. My vision for the league is that we have kids off the streets and out of trouble. This is the only way they could go on to college.*

- *Communication is the key to a successful community, and on the soccer field you see that communication between fathers and sons.*

to nearly one hundred participants. The result, of course, is a safer, cleaner, healthier community, not to mention the pride the participants feel in a job well done. The community is now empowered to take responsibility for maintaining their own community.

How do we measure the outcome/results of this particular project? We can't. We can't trace cause and effect between the cleanup project and an empowered, cleaner, healthier community, but from a systems perspective, we know that change has taken place. Such change is like dropping a stone into a pool of water. The outward ripple effect changes the condition of the pond.

The Oak View Youth Soccer League

In 2007, a group of Oak View fathers, led by Jose Luis Rodriquez, approached the then executive director, Alejandro Tovares, to get his thoughts on the development of a youth soccer league. This request would fill an important void in after-school programs for the girls and boys of the community as well as

> • *Through El Viento from over twelve years ago, I saw change, step by step, in the behavior in the children in our community.*

to provide a source of community involvement for the fathers as coaches.

Today, the league consists of over thirty teams, six hundred children, and thirty fathers. The soccer league is a source of pride and celebration within the community and has led to a number of outcomes related to the CWI, including health and exercise on the part of the players and a significant sense of empowerment on the part of the leaders and coaches. One more stone has been dropped into the pond.

I asked Iosefa to interview Jose Luis to obtain the background around the startup of the league in his own words. Jose Luis's English is limited, so Iosefa translated the interview and provided the literal translation in the following comments:

When we talk about grass-roots leadership, Jose Luis is a primary example of how one person, with a little help, is able to create change.

Leadership

Among the unintended consequences or outcomes of community initiatives is the emergence of a group of leaders who have taken responsibility for the cleanup and the soccer league. Those leaders, mothers, fathers, and grandparents, understand that the empowerment and renewal of the community is up to them. No one else, particularly from outside of the community, can do it to them or for them. This outcome is not included in any of our metrics, but does serve to illustrate the point that one cannot measure the things that are really important.

Medical and Dental Programs

In the spring of 2010, the Hoag Memorial Hospital Presbyterian provided the funding which enabled the Oak View Renewal Partnership to bring two major providers of health-care prevention, education, and treatment to the community. Once a month, mobile clinics operated by the Orange County Rescue Mission and Healthy Smiles for Kids of Orange County visit Oak View.

Working in cooperation with one another, the clinics bring to the community services that might not be available to our residents if they had to travel to visit fixed-site facilities some distance from Oak View. Each month upwards of forty patients are treated, with the result that the health condition of our families is clearly improving over time.

The Orange County Health Needs Assessment organization conducted a survey of the health status of our residents for the year ending February 2011. This assessment will establish a baseline that, over time, may be used to measure changes in the health status of our community. Again, we are incorporating assessment and measurement criteria into our community-change initiatives.

LESSONS LEARNED—WHAT I WOULD DO DIFFERENTLY

Good data are hard to find. Over the past three years, we have worked very hard to find the data that would help us measure the outcomes we sought to achieve. Our data gathering has been helped a lot by the fact that the Oak View community is completely contained within one census tract. However, there are a number of data elements that really are important but are not contained in the census reports. We should have worked with our community partners much earlier in the life of OVRP to put in place the data-collection processes required to evaluate or progress.

SUMMARY

We are trying to do something that has not been done successfully in other community-change efforts. That is, to set up a framework for analysis and to measure results. There are many studies that attempt to measure the effectiveness of specific programs and initiatives, but according to the research we have undertaken, there are no studies that measure the systemic impact of a combination of programs on the condition of a community.

We are plowing new ground here. Our business model or theory of change must be proved. Our Community Wellness Index, which attempts to provide a proof of concept, is also an experiment. As it is with anything experimental, we will experience failures and be forced to rethink our approach. We have no road map, and that is OK; we know that the existing pathways do not lead where we wish to go.

Exhibit VI-1a
Public Safety & Security

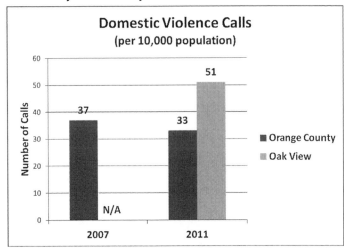

*Data for Oak View, 2007 not available.

Exhibit VI-1b
Public Safety & Security

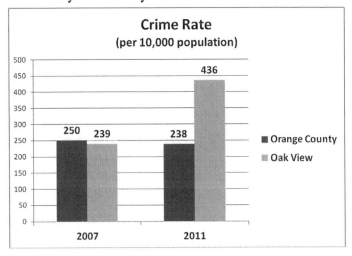

Exhibit VI-1c
Public Safety & Security

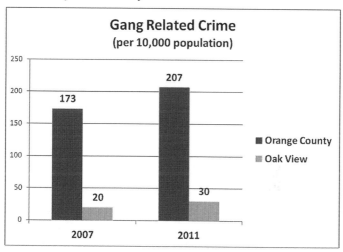

Exhibit VI-1d
Public Safety & Security

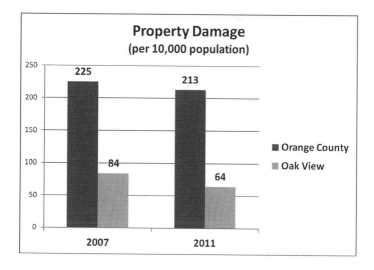

Exhibit VI-2a
Education

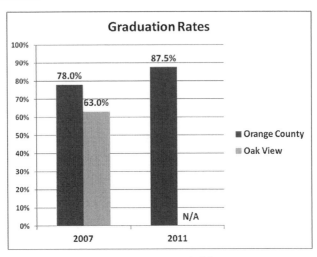

*Rate for Oak View, 2011 not available.

Exhibit VI-2b
Education

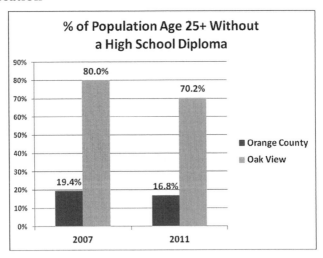

Exhibit VI-2c
Education

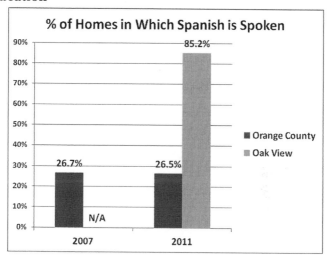

*Data for Oak View, 2007 not available.

Exhibit VI-3a
Health

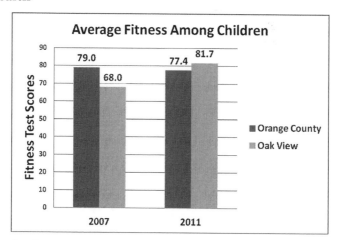

The higher the score, the greater the fitness rating.

Exhibit VI-3b
Health

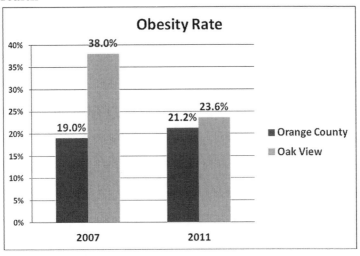

Exhibit VI-4a
Housing

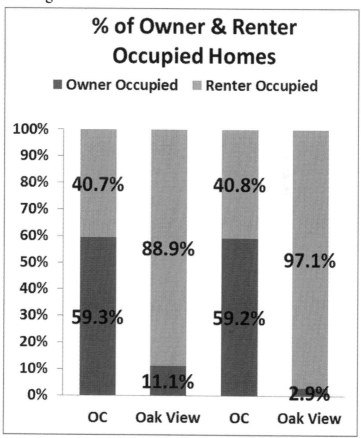

Exhibit VI-4b

Housing

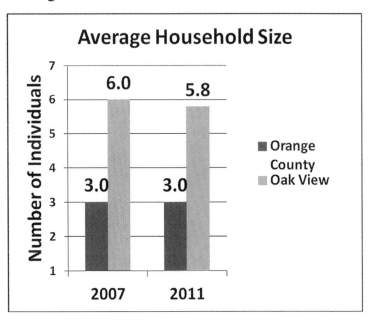

Exhibit VI-5a
Jobs/Income Security

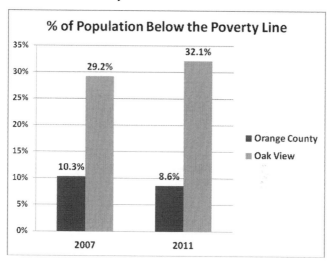

Exhibit VI-5b
Jobs/Income Security

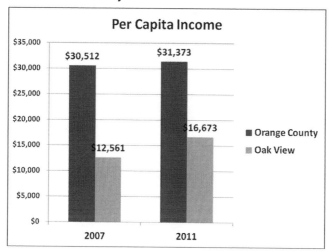

Exhibit VI-5c
Jobs/Income Security

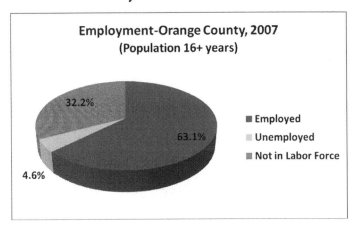

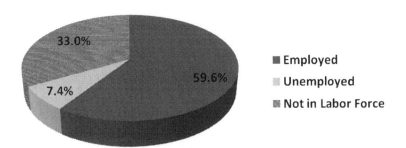

Exhibit VI-5d
Jobs/Income Security

Employment-Oak View, 2011
(Population 16+ years)

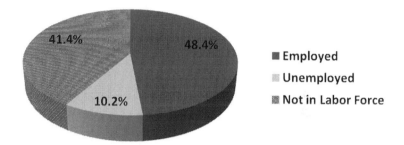

CHAPTER VII

The Public Safety And Security Gap—Civic Pride

The city changed from a strategy of containment to one of involvement.
—RON SHENKMAN

INTRODUCTION

The Community Environment Loop shown in Exhibit II-2 illustrates the urban hardship gaps between Oak View and the rest of Orange County. Narrowing the first gap listed, public safety and security, is a prerequisite to addressing all of the other urban hardship gaps.

Since the firebombing of the police substation in 1993, Oak View has become a safe, clean, secure place to raise a family, walk at night, and take pride in what has been accomplished. According to Lieutenant Gary Faust of the Huntington Beach Police Department, the drug dealers are gone, and while some gang activity is still present from time to time, there is nowhere near the problem that gangs once presented.

It doesn't matter how many social services are provided or what other resources are made available; if the residents of Oak View don't feel safe, empowerment and renewal will not take place. This point seems obvious on its face, but after having looked at other communities plagued by urban hardship, ten-foot fences topped with razor wire tell the story. The razor-wire fences are necessary to keep people out. There are no razor-wire fences in Oak View. They are unnecessary.

As I outlined in Chapter V, "Implementation—How Do We Get to Our Vision," the first step toward implementing a vision of empowerment is overcoming fear and creating trust, the action Joe Ames called "fear to trust." I believe that this first step was largely accomplished though the community policing initiative that began in 1993.

STRUCTURE AND PROCESS
Overarching Strategy
The firebombing may have been a blessing in disguise. The crisis resulting from that event had the direct effect of the city and the police department revisiting their strategy and adopting a new approach—community policing.

When the city of Huntington Beach moved from a strategy of containment to one of involvement, the groundwork for the road to empowerment and renewal began. As I pointed out in Chapter I, Oak View was a very bad place in the 1980s and early 1990s. The change in strategy on the part of the city enabled providers of services to feel comfortable and safe working in Oak View as well as enabling residents to feel confident in venturing out to utilize those services.

The strategy on the part of the city resulted in the police department appointing Lieutenant Luis Ochoa to head community policing in Oak View. In my opinion, based on my interviews with city officials and community-service professionals, Lieutenant Ochoa's activist role in becoming visible in the community, and relating to its residents, led to the direct result of a safer place. Cause and effect are very clear.

"New" Police Sub-station and Community Policing

Thanks to Lieutenant Ochoa's efforts with the owner of the shopping center on the corner of Beach and Slater, the new sub-station was opened in 1993. The new location created several unintended consequences that are worth mentioning here:

- Residents are more willing to visit the police station to report crimes or instances of domestic violence because they are less likely to be seen by other members of the community.

- The station represents less of a target for those random acts of violence that, while infrequent, occur in many communities.

Lieutenant Ochoa and his young patrolman, Gary Faust, led the way in "walking the beat" in the Oak View community. Luis and Gary, both Spanish speakers, got to know the residents as well as the "bad guys." They sent the "bad guys" to jail while sending a strong message to the community that there were police out there, not to be feared, but to be embraced as members of the community. Lieutenant Ochoa has retired and Gary Faust is now a lieutenant within the highest levels of the Huntington Beach Police Department, but their legacy carries on.

EXAMPLES OF WHAT IS WORKING
The Traffic Light

In 1996, a small child was killed by a vehicle on the dangerous, unmarked corner of Slater and Nichols. Of course, the community was outraged, primarily because of the death of the child, but also because this busy intersection had no stop sign or traffic light. Over the course of the next two years, community meetings and appeals to the city for a light met with very little support. There were many obstacles, including state approvals, complexity, and cost. Also, the priority for other intersections was higher than that established for Oak View. Perhaps most importantly, the community had no voice. There was no political representation of the residents.

All of this came to a head as the Oak View Renewal Partnership was becoming organized. Ron Shenkman of Rainbow Environmental Services, the Oak View Task Force, and OVRP took a lead role in petitioning the City Department of Public Works to raise the priority of the installation of the traffic light. We promised the community we would represent them and get the job done. And we did! The light was installed in 2005. The community saw that by working together they had a voice. The residents were becoming empowered.

Community Cleanup

As the Oak View Renewal Partnership was being formed, Zayda Garcia and I met with a small group to discuss what the members of the community felt would be important in bringing the community together around the subject of civic pride. I felt the answer would be the removal of graffiti and tagging. I was wrong. I had based my opinion on the experience of our model community, Market Creek Plaza in San Diego. What was different between Oak View and Market Creek Plaza was the fact that the residents of Market Creek Plaza were not afraid of the gangs and taggers. The members of the community with whom Zayda and I spoke were instead afraid of the possible actions of the taggers should they be observed removing graffiti. Instead, our little group suggested a community cleanup as a nonthreatening way to begin the process of instilling civic pride in our residents.

Our first Saturday cleanup crew consisted of Zayda as the leader in addition to the usual three to four mothers who tend to show up for everything, including Ruth Dominquez and Martha Jiménez. We also had an enthusiastic group of El Viento students. We supplied coffee, donuts, and T-shirts and got to work sweeping alleys. As we swept, it became obvious we were being watched. All the men of the community were sitting in their garages watching us work. I asked myself, "What is wrong with this picture?"

It was clear that we needed to make the project an effort shared by everyone in the community. As we say, everyone has to have some skin in the game. Over time and under the leadership of Zayda, Alejandro, Iosefa, Ruth, and Martha, the project took off. Today, the responsibility for the monthly cleanup rests with all of the organizations that serve the Oak View community, including:

- El Viento

- Community Service Programs (CSP)

- The library

- The Family Resource Center

- Ocean View High School

- Oak View Youth Soccer League

- Oak View Elementary School

The Oak View community is now a cleaner, healthier, safer place. Perhaps as important, the residents of the community have undertaken the responsibility for their own environment. The community is empowered with a sense of pride in the place they live.

Oak View Pride Day

Sponsored by the city, Rainbow Disposal, and CSP, Oak View Pride Day is a celebration of summer and the spirit of the community. The community is involved and invested in a cleanup, graffiti removal, and displays of art crated by the youth of Oak View. The Huntington Beach Police Department also displays, by their presence, the essence of community policing.

LESSONS LEARNED—WHAT I WOULD DO DIFFERENTLY

Of course, the primary lesson to be learned is that people must feel safe and free from fear. Thanks to the strategy of community policing, the children and families of Oak View do feel safe and we have begun the transition from fear to trust. I wasn't working in Oak View at the time of the firebombing of the police sub-station, but I can envision several responses on the part of the police department that would have had different consequences than those that we have experienced over the past eighteen years. First, the police could have responded with force that would have probably resulted in opposing force on the part of the gangs. Or, the city could have continued a policy of containment. Such isolation most likely would have inhibited any of the private social-services organizations from working in the community. The community would have been an armed camp into which outsiders would not enter.

In short, I would not do anything differently than what was done.

SUMMARY

During the course of my interviews with people who have served and worked in the Oak View community, there is one consistent theme—love! I didn't set out looking for love or asking questions having to do with feelings of any kind. The feelings just came out! The culture, behavior, and spirit of the community seem to invoke a set of feelings on the part of those who work in the community, including myself. I am not sure how many other communities bring about such feelings, but I do know that those feelings bring out the best in everyone. Our community partners deserve all the credit for working within the culture and leading with mutual respect, trust, and love.

The public safety and security and civic pride that characterize the very basis of community empowerment and renewal are alive and well in Oak View. With such a foundation in place, the remaining pillars of empowerment and renewal will be solidly built, which leads to the next gap to be narrowed: education.

CHAPTER VIII

The Education Gap—The Ticket To The Future

Give a man a fish and he won't starve for a day. Teach a man to fish and he won't starve for his entire life.
—CHINESE PROVERB

INTRODUCTION

Education, the second gap illustrated in the Community Environment Loop (Exhibit II-2), is in my opinion, the next important step in filling the remaining gaps. Helping narrow the education gap is the primary reason for the founding of the El Viento Foundation fifteen years ago. According to our Community Wellness Index (CWI), we have made some progress in graduation rates and in the percent of the population without a high-school education. These numbers are difficult to gather, but we continue to pursue improved methods of data collection and analysis.

Our One Square Mile community is served by a wonderful system of schools and a great branch of the Huntington Beach Library. As I mentioned in Chapter I, the role our schools and library play in the nurturing and development of our community is truly remarkable. Our schools see their roles as being way beyond the narrow, conventional view of teaching the basics and teaching "to the test."

I don't think for one moment that El Viento or the Oak View Renewal Partnership would even exist if it were not for the expanded view of the role of each school and, of course, the wonderful leadership that makes it all possible. Our principals, teachers, administrators, custodians, volunteers, and part-time lunch servers combine to serve our community with empathy, compassion, and love. In addition, the board of trustees of the Coast Community College District, the president of Golden West College, faculty, administration, and foundation, have played significant roles in supporting El Viento as well as the community-outreach and adult-education programs.

Referring back to our vision of empowerment as motivator for change, and the need to transition our community from fear to trust, I believe that the schools have helped make that transition, at least as far as education is concerned. Our parents certainly do not fear the schools, and with the leadership in place in all of the districts and schools, trust is alive and well.

From and education standpoint, the Oak View community has everything going for it—*except the education of our parents.*

STRUCTURE AND PROCESS
Overarching Strategy
Education is the key to everything! Lack of education is the barrier to everything! For example, health status and levels of education are highly correlated. Employment status and levels of education are similarly linked. After public safety and security, the highest priority urban hardship gap to be filled is that of education. Most important,

education provides our children and families with choices and the ability to make sound decisions. As we will see, the educational opportunities available to our community are enormous. Our goal is to empower our families to make the most of those opportunities.

The "center of gravity" of the Oak View community is the Oak View Elementary School. During the course of the past fifteen years that we have been working in Oak View, the school has been our home, and the principals, faculty, and staffs our closest friends, colleagues, and partners. The Oak View Elementary School has served as the base of operations for El Viento and the Oak View Renewal Partnership, providing space, technology, and infrastructure support, not to mention a place for me to go to work each morning. The trust of the community has been transferred from the school to El Viento and the Oak View Renewal Partnership. What a gift!

The System Is Working—Almost

The educational cycle from preschool to college is complete and available to all of the residents of the Oak View community, including these facilities:

- A preschool, funded by the Children and Families Commission of Orange County and administered by the Ocean View School District, is providing a great start for our kids and parents. The principal of the preschool, Joyce Horowitz, has done an outstanding job of creating a welcoming environment while delivering the skills necessary for our kids and their parents to learn. The adult-education facility at the preschool provides classes in parenting, English, and computers. Most importantly, research has shown that our kids are now ready to learn by the time they enter kindergarten.

- Oak View Elementary School, a California Distinguished School, is the next stop along our children's journey. This school, the home to 850 K-5 students, is really the focal point of the community. I conduct numerous tours of Oak View on behalf of El Viento and the Oak View Renewal Partnership and often find myself telling visitors that "Disneyland is not the happiest place on Earth; the Oak View Elementary School is the happiest place on Earth." The children are smiling and enthusiastic, reflecting the attitudes of the leadership and staff. The school is spotless, the walls are hung with posters celebrating progress, and the kids are doing well. Our kids are now on a trajectory for learning and for life, a course they would not be on were it not for the preparation they receive on the Oak View campus.

- The four middle schools of the Ocean View School District combine to take fifth graders from Oak View and turn them into students ready for high school. As is the case with middle school students in any community, these preteen years are tough for our kids and their teachers. In my view, the principals and teachers at Vista View, Marine View, Mesa View, and Spring View do a great job in helping the Oak View students assimilate among kids with different ethnic and demographic backgrounds. The journey continues.

- Ocean View High School is a wonderful place. About 650 of our Oak View students attend Ocean View. The principal, Dan Bryan, is a leader/coach who not only makes our kids feel good about themselves but also keeps raising the bar of academic achievement. Dan's view of the role of the school is as a valued resource for the entire community. I have gotten to know and respect him over the past two-and-a-half years since he arrived at Ocean View, and have come to call him "Dr. Yes." Dan says yes to nearly all of our requests for the school's assistance to the Oak View community, requests I will go into later in this chapter. The role of Ocean

View High School is much more than helping kids to graduate. Dan sees it as preparing our kids for college and for life.

- Golden West College is the next stop for many of the Oak View students. Led by President Wes Bryant and Director Margie Bunten, Foundation and Community Relations, the college has been a wonderful partner of El Viento and later the Oak View Renewal Partnership since the beginning of our work in Oak View. Our students have had access to the Puente program designed to bridge ethnic gaps, financial assistance, counseling, and a very supportive environment. However, our students are under a lot of pressures from many sources that combine to keep them from graduating, including the need to work, difficulty in getting classes, family obligations, early marriage, and pregnancy. Empowering our students to overcome those obstacles and to stay on course to finish and go on to four-years schools is the greatest challenge of El Viento and to narrowing the educational gap of our community.

- The Huntington Beach Adult School is led by Steve Curiel, a very capable young principal. Our greatest untapped resource is the facility for adult education on the Ocean View High School campus. In my view, our greatest educational obstacle is the lack of education on the part of our parents, who lack the basic education necessary to help their children to succeed in school. Many of our parents are illiterate in their native language, Spanish, as well as English. Most of our parents don't have the basic skills necessary to get any job above minimum wage.

    These two issues, education and jobs, are obviously, closely interlinked. Our parents desperately need jobs but, for a variety of reasons we will discuss, don't have the basic skills, including English, necessary to qualify for whatever jobs are available. I call this young parent segment of our population the "lost generation." If we are not able convince our age eighteen- to forty-year-old parents to take advantage of the educational opportunities afforded to them, not only will their children be deprived of a complete home-based education, but the parents will be forever lost to the economy.

- Oak View branch of the Huntington Beach Library. Under the direction of Claudia Locke, the library has provided an educational "home" for our community. For example, over 1500 of our residents have library cards, book circulation is three thousand books per month, the homework club works with two hundred kids per week, and the chess club has twenty members who show up every Friday afternoon. Claudia joined the Library at its inception seventeen years ago and is still excited about her role in the community. Claudia, a native of Peru, relates to the culture of the community and, like many others of us who serve Oak View, expresses a real love for the children and families.

The Family Literacy Program, under the direction of advisory board member Amy Crepau, provides parent tutoring, story times for parents and preschool children, and parent workshops of subjects of early childhood education, health, and parenting. Amy, like Claudia, has been in Oak View a long time and personally identifies with the needs, wants, and expectations of our children and their families.

Filling the Adult-education Gap—The Lost Generation

In 2010 there were 250,000 adults in Orange County over the age of twenty-five without a high-school diploma or its equivalent.

It is conceivable that if nothing changes, by the year 2035 that number may be as high as 600,000. Fully 25 percent of the work force in Orange County will be functionally illiterate. We will have a generation of adults who cannot compete in today's work environment much less the world of tomorrow.

The story of functional illiteracy is also the case in Oak View. Fully 25 percent of the adult population does not have a high-school education, and most do not speak English. This is a situation that simply cannot be tolerated. We cannot write off an entire generation and expect to empower and renew our community.

Jobs

The top priority of the Oak View Renewal Partnership, now, and for the foreseeable future, is that of jobs. But without adult education, there will be no jobs for the young people of our community. Therefore, we must combine our strategies of education with that of skills and English-language training to enable job creation to take place. We are working closely with Steve Curiel, principal of Ocean View Adult Education School, to create programs that will bring jobs-skills training to our workforce and to have that skills training actually lead to jobs.

There are numerous barriers to a program intended to integrate adult education with job creation, including the willingness of our young adults to take advantage of such programs. Our young parents, just as was the case with previous generations of parents and grandparents, are very busy either working at several low-paying jobs, looking for jobs, or just inclined not to take advantage of the programs being offered.

Referring back to Chapter II and the Service Delivery Value Chain (Exhibit II-3), we see our partners in education, facilitated in part by the Oak View Renewal Partnership, delivering very high-quality education and community service to our One Square Mile.

While most of these facilities were in place long before El Viento and OVRP, the community services have been enhanced and perhaps more closely linked as a direct result of OVRP being visible and involved. For example, the office of OVRP is located on the Oak View campus with the result that the principal and the community-outreach coordinator just walk down the hall to have a discussion with Iosefa or me. The office of El Viento is located on the campus of Golden West College with the result that our students have immediate access to the El Viento staff. In short, we are in the community we serve.

EXAMPLES OF WHAT IS WORKING
The El Viento Foundation
I have referred to El Viento many times during the course of this work. The mission and vision embraced by El Viento was really the beginning of our work in the Oak View community. My wife, an educator, and I, a businessperson and sailor, brought our passions and capabilities together to create an organization designed to give the students of the Oak View Elementary School an opportunity to go to college. Our long-range vision was the empowerment of the residents of the Oak View community. Collen Mensel, our chief executive officer, and Zayda Garcia, our chief operations officer, are now carrying the torch of sustainability.

The following is taken from a presentation I did ten years ago in an effort to communicate what I called "The El Viento Story":

Our Vision—We seek to make a difference—to leave a legacy—for the children, the families, and the community of Oak View and Huntington Beach.

Our Mission—El Viento will provide children and young adults with opportunities for success in life as responsible citizens though a long-term relationship based on leadership, mutual trust and respect, exemplary character, teamwork, learning, and skill building.

We used the experience of sailing as a metaphor for life as we sought to provide our students and parents with choices and the skills, knowledge, and wisdom necessary to make good decisions from the choices available.

The quotation below is taken from a poem by Ella Wheeler Wilcox, poet and journalist (1851–1919):

"One ship sails East, and another West, by the self-same winds that blow, 'tis the set of the sails and not the gales, that tells the way to go."

Our Goals:

- *El Viento uses sailing and sea-related activities to teach life lessons.*

- *El Viento focuses on physical, educational, and character-building activities through partnerships with schools, colleges, development organizations, and other community constituencies that share our vision.*

- *El Viento will help our students and their families to manage the path to educational achievement.*

- *Over time, the success of El Viento will be measured by the growth and fulfillment of our participants.*

El Viento has been a successful model for educational opportunity in Oak View and in Orange County. Each year we begin with a group of twenty-five fourth graders and stay with them though middle school, high school, and the first two years of college. Those students who stay in the program and graduate from high school are awarded with a two-year scholarship to a community college. We have educated several hundred students and now have forty in college and many who have graduated from two- and four-year colleges and universities.

The El Viento Foundation also served as an incubator for the startup of the Oak View Renewal Partnership in 2007. That is, El Viento provided "seed capital" for early operating expenses of OVRP as well acting as a fiscal intermediary until OVRP became a tax-exempt public benefit corporation. El Viento is now among the many organizations that are included in the Provider Component of Chapter II.

Viva

El Viento introduced an important educational component to the Oak View Elementary School in 2009: Viva Technology, a science, technology, and math (STEM) initiative sponsored by Great Minds in STEM, based in Los Angeles. Each year, engineers from many of the aerospace and technology firms in Southern California descend on the Oak View Elementary School campus to conduct hands-on scientific experiments and classes designed to stimulate the interests of our fifth graders in science and math. On the evening before the major event, a special program is conducted for the parents of the students to introduce the program and to emphasize the importance of science and math to the future of their children.

As a follow-up to the Viva program, El Viento is also providing STEM tutoring to our fifth graders though a special grant from the Draper Family Foundation and Edwards Life Sciences. Our elementary-school tutor, Jesse Rothman, provides hands-on experiments one Monday afternoon per month. Watching those experiments provides a STEM experience for all ages.

The Ocean View High School Business Academy

Through the leadership of Roger Keating, the business academy has provided a great academic and cultural bridge between our Oak

View students and the high school. All of the El Viento students are welcomed into the business academy during their sophomore year and take part in Roger's valuable tutoring, coaching, and mentoring. In addition, many other Oak View students take part in the business academy, giving them valuable accounting, marketing, human resources, and business operational skills. Roger also makes our students feel valued, important, and successful.

The Oak View Renewal Partnership Advisory Board

The Oak View Renewal Partnership has been truly fortunate to have serving on our advisory board many leaders of the Huntington Beach educational community. These individuals do not just give their names to our efforts; they "show up." This linkage between our educational leaders and our community is critical in shaping public policy, providing experience, and serving as ambassadors of our organizations. I am listing the following individuals who were extremely supportive in the early days of El Viento and OVRP as well as those leaders who continue in their footsteps:

- Dr. William Vega, retired chancellor, Coast Community College District

- Dr. Kenneth Yglesias, retired chancellor, Coast Community College District, and former president, Golden West College

- Ms. Margie Bunten, director, Foundation & Community Relations

- Dr. Wes Brian, president, Golden West College

- Ms. Karen Catabeijan, former principal, Oak View Elementary School

- Dr. James Tarwater, former superintendent, Ocean View School District

- Ms. Fran Andrade, former community liaison, Oak View Elementary School

- Ms. Sherri Medrano, community liaison, Oak View Elementary School

- Dr. Van Riley, retired superintendent, Huntington Beach Union High School District

These leaders trusted us and in turn conveyed that trust to the parents of Oak View. As I indicated previously, without that trust, there would be no El Viento or Oak View Renewal Partnership.

Today's leaders, following in the footsteps of their predecessors include:

- Joyce Horowitz, former principal, Oak View Elementary School, and current principal, Oak View Preschool

- Dr. William Loose, superintendent, Ocean View School District

- Ms. Laura Dale-Pash, principal, Ocean View Elementary School

- Mr. Dan Bryan, principal, Ocean View High School

- Dr. Gregory Pluko, superintendent, Huntington Beach Union High School District

- Ms. Debbie Cotton, member of the board of the Ocean View School District

- Mr. Steve Curiel, principal, Huntington Beach Adult School

- Mr. Robert Tapia, community liaison, Ocean View High School

There are many other who could be on this list. We have received the trust of teachers, custodians, administrative staff, volunteers, and a whole host of involved individuals who make up a community.

Those I listed above have made closing the education "gap" a priority in their roles and leaders and as individuals.

LESSONS LEARNED—WHAT I WOULD DO DIFFERENTLY

The lessons of cooperation and collaboration have been well learned. No ship sails on its own bottom, so to speak. In a systems world, we are all connected and our efforts, interdependent. More than any other community I have researched, Oak View is truly a community that is connected. The Oak View Renewal Partnership has built on that connectivity to become a catalyst for change. There is much work to be done to narrow the education gap, but the foundation of mutual respect and trust has been built. Perhaps more importantly, the "fear to trust" barrier has been overcome.

We have also learned that a community must have a center, a focal point. That center may be a school, a community center, a Boys and Girls Club, a YMCA, or whatever organization is willing to step up to the task. In the case of Oak View, Oak View Elementary School has been that center for over twenty-five years. Our community would not be where it is today without the generation of leaders who have provided that center.

We have not done as good a job as we should have in involving the parents in the education of their children. While we have parent involvement in the schools, including Parent Teacher Organizations, serving as volunteers, etc. we have not provided the parents with the tools they require to help their children to read, assist with homework, and to take a real interest in the day to day learning process.

As I review the literature on education, I am made aware of the critical role of parents in reading to their children, regardless of language, and inquiring about how well their children are doing and what problems they face. This shortcoming is understandable in that many of our parents are illiterate in Spanish and can't help their children in the home, while others are working multiple jobs and are just not available when their children need help.

Also, the culture of our community is also one that tends to leave teaching to the teachers, as compared to other cultures that take a more proactive role in their children's education. I believe these problems may be addressed though programs of adult education, including English as a second language, computer literacy, and the role of parenting in children's education. In particular, I believe that we must communicate to our parents the need for high expectations for the academic performance of their children and themselves. In the absence of high expectations, our teachers can only do so much.

SUMMARY

From the beginnings of El Viento to today, we have come a long way toward narrowing the education gap. Our scores, however measured, have improved significantly over these past fifteen years, but the best must be yet to come if we are to see an empowered and renewed community within the next generation of Oak View residents. Our adults must become educated and get jobs. Our students must be encouraged by their parents to stay in school and to go on to college. Oak View must become the model that will serve as an example of what is possible when the community and the schools work together to change lives.

CHAPTER IX

The Health And Wellness Gap—Why It Matters

We must move from a culture of emergency-room treatment to one of prevention and education.
—HEALTHY SMILES FOR KIDS OF ORANGE COUNTY

INTRODUCTION

The third gap illustrated in Exhibit II-2, the Community Environment Loop, is that of health. Narrowing the health gap through education and prevention versus treatment may present the greatest challenge of all. According to our Community Wellness Index (CWI), we have made some progress regarding the average fitness among children and in childhood obesity, but as we will see later, issues of poor health among our adult population are of great concern. Perhaps more importantly, as we think about the barriers to empowerment and our "fear to trust" model, I believe that we have a long way to go in removing the fear barrier in health care. Except in cases of emergency, our families are often fearful of engaging our system of health care. The reasons for this fear are many and varied, but no matter what, those fears must be understood and overcome if we are to be successful in empowering a healthy community.

The connection between health, education, and economic status has been well established. Families must be sufficiently educated to access the health system, yet such education is not often available due to reasons of health. Children can't learn if they are in pain. Workers with chronic illness cannot find employment. Programmatic initiatives that focus on education are not as effective as they could be because of the health status of the recipients of such programs. Similarly, programs focused on health often do not take into consideration issues of education. Unfortunately, our system health care places a focus on treatment rather than education or prevention. In addition, the access to care is limited by cost and immigration status. All of these issues and obstacles must be understood and taken into consideration in the development of a healthy community.

STRUCTURE AND PROCESS
Overarching Strategy
According the study conducted by the Orange County Health Needs Assessment, with the exception of emergency services, our families simply will not use services that are not located in the Oak View community. Free or low-cost health-care education, prevention, and treatment services must be brought to Oak View in order to deal with the combined issues of fear, access, and affordability.

The health-care strategy for the Oak View community has been undertaken in multiple phases:

- Providing nutrition, healthy eating and exercise programs in schools

- Enabling short-term use of mobile medical and dental clinics

- Development of partnerships that will result in the creation of an on-site facility

- Making health insurance available whenever possible

In February 2010, Hoag Memorial Hospital Presbyterian financed our bringing to the community two mobile clinics on a once-a-month basis: Healthy Smiles for Kids of Orange County, a mobile dental facility, and the Hurt Family Health Clinic, a mobile medical facility. During the nearly two years since the introduction of the clinics, over three hundred adults and children have been treated by the two facilities. During the first year of operation, the Orange County Health Needs assessment program identified a wide variety of chronic health problems among those patients who visited the facility, including these:

- Symptoms of stress and anxiety, including high blood pressure

- Diabetes

- Anemia

- Heart disease

These diseases, of course, lend themselves to community medicine programs of education and prevention.

Concurrent with the short-term mobile clinic program, we are also investigating, with Hoag Hospital, Ocean View High School, and the Share Our Selves (SOS) community clinic, the feasibility of placing an on-site health modular unit on the campus of the Ocean

View High School. The facility would be financed in part by Hoag Memorial Hospital Presbyterian, and managed by the SOS clinic. Funding in these difficult economic times is, of course, a major issue, but our planning work continues.

The population density of the Oak View community, upwards of twenty people living in a two-bedroom apartment, also lends itself to the health problems experienced by the residents. In the words of Allen Baldwin, executive director of the Orange County Community Housing Corporation, who will be introduced in Chapter XI:

> Since we will experience high-occupancy (some say "overcrowded") housing in this neighborhood for the foreseeable future, there is a need to establish property management and community protocols that will keep our families safe and healthy with many people under one roof. There are issues of respiratory problems, molestation, and abuse that are more likely in these conditions than would be normal with traditional occupancies.

Allen's insight is systems thinking at its best. We can't deal with just health without dealing with education and housing.

EXAMPLES OF WHAT IS WORKING
Healthy Smiles for Kids of Orange County

In 2000, the school nurse serving the Oak View Elementary School, Carol Kanode, brought to my attention the oral health condition of the children of Oak View. Carol said, "Jack, for all of your good intentions, these kids will not even get to high school, much less graduate and go on to college." My response was "Thanks, but what are you talking about?" The nurse went on to describe the cultural issue she called the "Bottle Baby Disease." In effect, babies are put to bed with a bottle of milk or juice in their mouths, which ultimately provides a breeding ground for bacteria that infect their gums, teeth, and overall mouth. The children's teeth are rotted before they are even developed. In addition, habits of tooth brushing as well as the presence of vast amounts of sugar in the diet destroy the primary teeth as well as the secondary teeth as they develop. The decay and the bacteria present in the children's mouths are highly toxic and contagious. Such conditions may actually lead to death.

Children who are in constant pain often do not realize that the pain is not a normal condition and go on to demonstrate attention-deficit behavior, have difficulty concentrating and learning, and miss many days of school. In addition, the appearance of rotten teeth results in low self-esteem and antisocial behavior. This children's disease is actually more prevalent than diabetes or asthma.

I asked Carol what we should do to help the El Viento kids escape this cycle of poor oral health and education risk. Her response was that there were no facilities in Orange County to care for children with no dental insurance and that; in fact, there were fewer than fifty pediatric dentists in all of Orange County. Carol had learned of the an organization in the city of Inglewood, up in Los Angeles County, known as the Children's Dental Center, that treated kids without insurance and provided facilities and programs of education and prevention. I said, "Let's go", and we drove to Inglewood.

The Children's Dental Center was a dream come true. It was exactly what we were looking for. The center, founded by the father of a nationally renowned dentist, Dr. Cherilyn Sheets, is a clinic designed just for kids. The dental chairs, sinks, learning stations, and graphic designs are all kid friendly. Children and their parents are educated in proper oral hygiene, treatment is provided on a sliding scale according to ability to pay, and prevention is the order of the day.

Soon after our visit to the Children's Dental Center, El Viento began a program of bussing our kids to Inglewood for education and treatment. Most of the El Viento students had severe decay and disease issues requiring multiple visits for treatment.

Seeing the unmet need for helping children in Orange County, Dr. Sheets made contact with the newly formed Children and Families Commission of Orange County. The California Prop 10, First 5 Initiative provided funds to each county to deal with issues faced by children and families during the first five years of a child's life. The initiative provided for preschool learning, maternal education, and clinical services. Working with Michael Ruane, the executive director of the Children and Families Commission of Orange County, Dr. Sheets and her colleagues developed a feasibility study for a children's oral health program to be financed by the commission.

Following the adoption of the feasibility study, Dr. Sheets introduced me to Mike Ruane, who asked me to help take the initiative to another level, including working with Dottie Andrews, whom I introduced in Chapter IV, in the creation of a formal business plan and budget and recruiting of a board of directors. The meeting with Mike Ruane in Dr. Sheets's office led to a ten-year relationship with Mike and Dottie and what would become Healthy Smiles for Kids of Orange County.

We went on to form a great board of directors, hiring Sandra Bolton as executive director. Under Sandra's leadership a children's dental clinic was built in Garden Grove and a network of dental clinics was created, which now serve nearly half of the children who live below the federal poverty level in Orange County. After five years of building the organization, Sandra has been succeeded by Liz Bear, who came on board two years ago and is continuing build the organization and shape its future notwithstanding the funding issues that accompany the "Great Recession."

A major chapter in that history is the relationship between Healthy Smiles and the Oak View Elementary School. Healthy Smiles provides dental screening and the application of fluoride varnish to children's teeth as well as the education of parents in proper oral hygiene. In addition, the Healthy Smiles Mobile unit provides once a month on-site dental services to the children of the Oak View community. We no longer have to bus our kids to Inglewood for dental treatment.

Children's Health Initiative of Orange County

In early 2007, my colleague Dottie Andrews, who had moved on to the St. Joseph's Hospital, called to ask if there would be any interest on the part of the community in what was called the "100 Percent Campaign," a project designed to provide health insurance for all of the kids of Oak View. I jumped at the opportunity to bring the campaign to Oak View with the result that during the 2006–2007 school year all of the children and their siblings had health coverage provided by:

- Medi-Cal for children and pregnant women

- Medi-Cal for adults

- Healthy Families

- CaliforniaKids

- Kaiser Permanente Child Health Plan (KPCHP)

Since the recession of 2008–2010, funding for many of the programs was eliminated, but from time to time, as funding becomes available, we work closely with the staff of the Family Resource Center to enroll as many eligible children as funds permit.

OC in Motion

In the fall of 2006, another colleague, Barbara Shipnuck, then director of Community Relations for Kaiser Permanente and an

El Viento board member, called to invite OVRP to take part in a program to become known as OC in Motion. The project was introduced by the Robert Wood Johnson Foundation to combat the epidemic in childhood obesity. The leadership of the project came under the direction of Kirsten Thompson, director of the YMCA Community Services Branch. The vision of the project was to "eliminate childhood obesity in our lifetime." The goals of the program were as follows:

- To increase awareness of the importance of physical activity in kids (sixty minutes/day) and adults (thirty minutes/day)

- To encourage public policy that supports the access/availability of open space within our communities

- To decrease the instances of diabetes and other related illnesses

I was invited to serve on a steering committee for the project and continued to do so for the next two years. During the course of that period, OC in Motion was introduced to the schools serving Oak View as well as being integrated into the various fitness programs already in place. Unfortunately, the YMCA of Orange County redirected its efforts in 2008 and the program was eliminated; however, an integral part of the program, Harvest of the Month, continues to the present time in the Oak View Elementary School.

An Oak View health education post-survey synopsis was conducted by our evaluation organization, ETI, in April 2008, with the result that the children and parents surveyed overwhelmingly agreed that they were more aware of healthy eating and exercise, and indeed, were exercising more and eating healthier than was previously the case.

Since all of the programs undertaken by OVRP and our community partners are connected and related in a cause-and-effect manner, the following initiatives described elsewhere also have had important impacts on the health of our children and their families:

- HB Mercado Certified Farmers Market

- The Oak View Soccer League

- The Oak View Girls Running Club

- El Viento swimming and sailing programs

- FRC Health Access and Family Advocate

- CSP recreational programs

- School readiness programs

SUMMARY

Our partners in Oak View have made great progress toward satisfying the health needs of our children. From school-lunch programs to nutrition and fitness classes, to mobile and school-based clinics, we have made great strides in the areas of awareness, education, prevention, and treatment over the past ten years. The major issues we face have to do with the health of our adult population. Issues of fear, culture, youth, cost, and immigration status are great barriers to community health. Hopefully the funding for a school-based, permanent facility is in the not-too-distant future.

CHAPTER X

The Jobs Gap—Economic Freedom

Work gives life meaning.
—SUMILKO TAN

INTRODUCTION

Our fourth gap, illustrated in Exhibit II-2, the Community Environment Loop, is that of jobs. Meaningful, valued work is at the heart of community renewal and empowerment. Jobs are also at the heart of our "fear to trust" imperative.

We really don't know the unemployment rate in Oak View. It may not be knowable. What we do know is that for reasons of education, immigration status, and health, many potential workers are standing on street corners or in the parking lots of the "big box" stores looking for work. I estimate that we have somewhere around one thousand men and women in our community who are actively seeking work, which would yield about a 50 percent unemployment rate among adults over eighteen years of age.

Jobs, which empower the individual, provide resources to sustain the family and the community. Jobs, leading to a freedom of choice, are essential for our families to gain respect and to overcome fear, stereotyping, and prejudice.

STRUCTURE AND PROCESS
Overarching Strategy
The Oak View Renewal Partnership is committed to helping our community to narrow the economic gap through the acquisition of resources required to provide adult education and workforce training. We are working with our community partners to design programs to overcome illiteracy and to provide skills that will produce greater-than-minimum-wage jobs. We are also designing our social-enterprise strategy, as outlined in Chapter XII, to provide work for members of our community.

Of course, all of this is easier said than done. The facilities for adult education are available, but the students aren't. We must work to attract students by providing incentives, including the prospect of jobs, at the conclusion of their training programs. We simply can't ask busy, stressed parents to make time to take part in training that does not have near-term benefits.

At the present time, we are partnering with the Huntington Beach Adult School, which has just completed a beautiful structure on the campus of our local high school, to tailor programs to meet the needs of our customers. Using this facility as a base, we intend to work closely with organizations such as Taller San Jose in Santa Ana, Goodwill Industries, and Working Wardrobes to provide our students with the skills required by our local industries and professions.

EXAMPLES OF WHAT IS WORKING
Rainbow Environmental Services

I thought it would be useful to start our series of job-creation examples with an organization that is working and has been an important factor in the economic life our community for over a generation. I often tell people that if Rainbow didn't exist we would have to invent it. Employing over sixty workers from Huntington Beach, including twenty-four from Oak View, Rainbow is an employee stock ownership plan (ESOP), which means that the company is owned by its employees. Our residents have an economic interest in the organization that provides them with skills training and meaningful work.

I have introduced Ron Shenkman, chairman of Rainbow, elsewhere in this journal, but for this commentary, it is important to note the tremendous contribution Ron and his colleagues have made to our community. The company has made major capital investments in the infrastructure of the organization, which have benefitted the community in many ways, not to mention the stability of the workforce.

Goodwill Industries

We are working closely with a unit of Goodwill Industries MicroEnterprise Project to provide training for a selected set of our community leaders. The program, known as Future Business Owners, has provided onsite training during the course of a twelve-week course to teach entrepreneurship designed to enable students to be in a position to take responsibility for our social-enterprise endeavors. A ceremony celebrating our first graduating class took place on December 6, 2011, on the occasion of our annual board luncheon.

We are also working with Goodwill to provide not only training but also job development in our community. Goodwill will be instrumental in seeking employment opportunities for our residents who complete their training programs.

Taller San Jose—St. Joseph's Workshop

Taller San Jose is a well-known Santa Ana, California, organization whose mission is to help their students gain the skills they need to secure above-minimum-wage skilled positions in local industries and professions. Taller San Jose provides unskilled and unemployed young adults with a sixteen-week paid training program that focuses on:

- Medical Careers Academy

- Office Careers Academy

- Taller Tech Construction Academy

Taller San Jose also sponsors a social-enterprise program that provides affordable housing rehabilitation services called Hope Builders.

Our goal in working with Taller San Jose is one of tailoring the programs they provide to the needs of our customers and our industrial and professional employers. Whether we send our students to Santa Ana or create a "sub-station" of Taller San Joes in Oak View remains to be seen, but the model is one we feel has merit for our community and its needs.

Working Wardrobes

Led by founder/CEO Jerri Rosen, Working Wardrobes is an Orange County–based organization designed to help men and women enter the workforce. I have watched Working Wardrobes for the past decade as it has grown and embraced a very successful social-enterprise model, while at the same time providing career training, job-placement assistance, and wardrobe services. Working Wardrobes has partnered with El Viento to provide job-assistance services to our graduates and is now poised to work with the Oak

View Renewal Partnership to assist in empowering our residents to achieve meaningful work.

Huntington Beach Adult School

Working closely with Principal Steve Curiel, we hope to build a pipeline between Oak View and the Huntington Beach Adult School located at the edge of our community on Gothard Avenue. We expect to fill that pipeline with adults from our community who are willing to work hard to change their condition. Steve, who sits on our advisory board, is anxious to work with our other community partners to identify individuals who need the skills and language capabilities to seek meaningful work. Steve recognizes that our families simply do not have the time or resources to attend classes that do not lead directly to jobs.

LESSONS LEARNED—WHAT I WOULD DO DIFFERENTLY

We started the Oak View Renewal Partnership in 2005, just prior to the "Great Recession" of 2008. Job creation, while important, did not seem to have the priority that is now the case. We should have realized that job creation is important in good times as well as bad times. We should have realized that English-language and work-related skills would provide an economic base for our community at all times.

Today, the economic condition faced by our residents is much more critical than it was five or six years ago. And, of course, it is much more difficult today to provide the assistance and to identify the employment opportunities that would have been the case had we started earlier. All that said, our number-one priority for the future of the Oak View Renewal Partnership is that of leadership development and job creation though adult education.

SUMMARY

The "heavy lifting" around job creation is just getting underway. We have very little to report at this writing except to say that we now have placed the creation of jobs as our highest priority and are working with all of our partners to provide opportunities for our residents. I have high hopes that the graduates of our recent Goodwill Industries program will find jobs though our social-enterprise initiatives, including the HB Mercadeo Certified Farmers Market and Emoción, our promotional-products business.

CHAPTER XI

The Housing Gap—Safe, Affordable, And Healthy Places To Raise A Family

---

We knew housing alone wasn't going to change lives.
—ALLEN BALDWIN

INTRODUCTION

Our fifth "gap" illustrated in Exhibit II-2, the Community Environment Loop, is housing.

> *I think we must accept the fact that we may not find short-term solutions to the housing gap. That said, there is still a lot that we can do to alleviate the impact of the density with which our residents live. In addition, there is a great deal we must do to overcome the fear that our customers face in dealing with property owners and managers. Fear must be transitioned to trust if we are to empower our residents and enable them to feel safe and to live in a healthy environment.*

The above quotation from Allen Baldwin, executive director of Orange County Community Housing Corporation (OCCHC), was given to me during an interview I conducted with Allen in preparing this chapter. Allen, a career real-estate developer, designed the OCCHC in 1977, not just to develop affordable-housing programs but to also change lives through education. I have known Allen since the beginnings of the Oak View Renewal Partnership, and came to realize that we had much in common around the issues of making difference at a community level.

Narrowing the housing gap may be the most economically challenging of all our gaps. Land costs along the Coast of Orange County make affordable housing, without subsidies of one kind or another, virtually impossible. With land costs in the general vicinity of Oak View approaching $1 million per acre, and apartment costs of nearly $150,000 per unit, with very little land available and government grants drying up, not much change is going to take place in population density.

Declining property values in our community have introduced yet another complication to efforts to narrow the housing gap. Many of those property owners who bought their units during the "boom" days now find themselves facing foreclosure or short sales on properties now "underwater." The response on the part of some property owners is to raise rents and reduce maintenance costs. Both of these factors, of course, worsen the living conditions for the tenants. More families must now squeeze into these units in order to pay the rent while a reduction in maintenance, in particular plumbing systems, presents ever-increasing health problems

To briefly review the demographics of Oak View, we have nearly ten thousand individuals, three thousand families, living in just over one thousand units, within two census block groups equaling about 20 percent of a square mile. Property costs, as reflected in apartment rents, result in two to three families of five or more to a family living in one unit in order to afford monthly rent averaging $1,500 per unit. Our families, representing two to three generations of Oak View residents, are willing to put up with the consequences of such density in order to take advantage of the facilities and services available in the community as well as multi-generations of family history.

STRUCTURE AND PROCESS
Overarching Strategy—Short-term

The vision of the Oak View Renewal Partnership is empowerment of our *current* residents and the renewal of our *current* physical structures. Our business model, or theory of change, does not include forcing families to leave Oak View and tearing down and rebuilding higher-priced apartment units.

I have witnessed the results of gentrification, that is, the so-called transforming of a rundown or aging neighborhood into a more prosperous one, e.g. though investment in remodeling buildings or houses. The outcome of gentrification not only changes the condition of the physical structure of the community; it forces out the families who can no longer afford to live in "their" community. The community and its residents are exchanged for something new and different. The families who are forced to leave the community end up creating denser communities elsewhere.

We may only slightly close our housing gap. We may do well only though making do with what we have, making conditions more livable for our current residents, and making the investments our property owners more secure. We intend to focus on the outcomes of density, particularly in terms of public safety and security and health. By working with our property owners, including the Orange County Community Housing Corporation, Jamboree Housing, and other property managers such as Trident Property Management, we hope to renew the community from within without destroying it from without.

Overarching Strategy—Longer-term

Prior to the "Great Recession" of 2008, a group of our community partners came together to design a strategy we came to know as the Bridge to the Future. We brought together experts in the following areas:

- Public policy

- Community development

- Urban development and land-use planning

- Real-estate development

- Finance

- Affordable housing

- City of Huntington Beach, Department of Economic Development

- Retail, including grocery

We held many meetings over the course of six months during 2008, which resulted in the development of a comprehensive urban plan for the Oak View community. We went so far as to integrate the plans we developed with those being developed by the city of Huntington Beach. Capital was available during the period prior to the run up of the real estate crash of 2008. Using Market Creek Plaza in San Diego as our model, we contemplated raising enough capital to acquire property along Beach Boulevard to be developed into facilities that would fit the needs of the community, including:

- A Hispanic grocery store

- A medical clinic

- Possible outlets for the sale of products created by members of the community

We further envisioned acquiring several parcels of underused real estate for further development into multi-level apartments with underground parking. Our preliminary feasibility study indicated that if we built could build up to three levels of affordable housing, we could relieve some of the congestion and pressure on some of the existing properties.

Again, using Market Creek Plaza as a model, we planned to create a cooperative form of organization that would hold title to the real estate and that would, in effect, be owned by the members of the community.

Our vision of community renewal came to a crashing halt at the end of 2008. I believe that the Bridge to the Future, or at least parts of that plan, will serve as a basis for the long-term renewal of Oak View. The Oak View section of the Beach Boulevard corridor between Edinger and Slater is just too valuable for the current businesses, including a junkyard, a sandwich shop, and a tire and battery facility. At some point, the community of Oak View will be opened up to face out on Beach Boulevard and to become integrated with other business along that corridor. Our Bridge to the Future document provides a graphic presentation of our vision of renewal.

EXAMPLES OF WHAT IS WORKING
Orange County Community Housing Corporation

I introduced Allen Baldwin, a member of our advisory board earlier in this chapter. The OCCHC owns and manages forty-four units in Oak View which are great examples of not only providing safe, affordable, and healthy places to raise a family, but also delivering the social services that change lives, including college-awareness programs such as STEP UP, after-school tutoring, and family mentoring. The capital employed by the OCCHC was made available through Housing and Urban Community Development Block Grants (CDBG), the type of funding no longer available in the amounts required to acquire and renovate affordable-housing units.

Jamboree Housing
Jamboree Housing, with a mission similar to the OCCH, provides nineteen apartments in Oak View together with the social services which are required by either block grants or tax credits. Jamboree has a great reputation for providing high-quality facilities that are well managed.

Oak View Property Owners Association
Led by Rich Edmonston, a founding board member of the Oak View Renewal Partnership, much is being done to improve the quality of life for our residents while maintaining rental rates that are as affordable as possible given the cost of real estate and the required maintenance of the properties. Rich has owned and maintained properties in Oak View for over twenty-five years and has a reputation for listening to his tenants and providing them with well-maintained, secure properties. In fact, one of our community gardens was developed and is being maintained by the tenants of one of Rich's properties.

Another member of the Oak View Property Owners Association, Katherine Johansen, director of Trident Property Management L.P., brings yet another perspective to our issue of housing—that of public safety and security and health. Katie as she is known, was educated in the health and nutrition field and worked for many years as a nutritionist educator at the University of California, Irvine. Katie took over the family real-estate management business upon the passing of her father and now runs a company with extensive holdings in multi-tenant properties in Orange County. During my interview with Katie, it became very clear that her interest in the well-being of her tenants was on a par with the economic well-being of her company. In Katie's view, her properties are more valuable if her tenants feel safe and are healthy.

I asked Katie to add some of her thoughts to this journal. Her response was to share with my readers the mission statement of her organization together with her approach to enhancing the quality of life for the residents. I have reproduced her thoughts in the following paragraphs:

Trident Property Management LP/
Solteros Apartments LP Mission Statement

Trident Property Management L.P. and its employees seek to provide the highest quality of safe and affordable living to residents, including responding quickly to problems and demonstrating a commitment to treat residents ethically, fairly, and with respect, and in accordance with all local, state and federal regulations regarding equal opportunity housing, including all pertinent housing and business practice legislation. Trident Property Management L.P. employees seek to maintain a progressive, innovative atmosphere that encourages the public to willingly enter into rental agreements and to maintain a high quality of life, within their scope, for every resident. In addition, Trident Property Management L.P. is committed to providing a safe and healthy work environment for all employees and requires employees to work together and to communicate effectively to achieve this goal.

We've owned and managed this property since 1975 and seen many changes in the neighborhood around us, and our property seems very out of character for the current community's needs. We offer studio and one-bedroom apartments, hence the name "solteros" or "bachelor" or "single male". Many of the programs and activities in the OakView community do not reach our community. Further, in our effort to reach our goals and adhere to our mission, we have a very strict occupancy standard. We do not allow more than two persons per bedroom per apartment. Unlike our neighboring landlords, we believe that high density leads to stress on the residents and the community, and burdens the property so that it compromises the environment and quality of life, and increases the likelihood of service interruptions. Landlords who do allow any number of residents to reside in their apartments find themselves with much more property damage, which means the entire area declines in value, potentially reinforcing to residents that no one cares.

We have been an active part in the Oak View Property Owner's Association, and have worked with the city of Huntington Beach through their police , code enforcement, economic development and public works departments in our effort to maximize resources to improve the quality of life for our residents.

The Oak View Property Owners Association, with the leadership of Rich and Katie, promises to become even more involved with the empowerment and renewal of our community though the hosting of community forums for our residents on subjects that include the responsibilities of renters and owners, health-related matters, and possibly, immigration. To me this is what the word "partnership" is all about.

LESSONS LEARNED—WHAT I WOULD HAVE DONE DIFFERENTLY?

Given the cost of real estate and the decline in either tax-sponsored or grant-funded projects, there is probably not much more we could have done, even with the benefit of hindsight. What we might have worked on earlier, similar to the community cleanup project, was educating families in the upkeep of their apartments and the responsibilities of property owners. I think that our strategy of making do with what we have could have been greatly enhanced by working with the property owners and tenants to make the units more livable.

Over the longer term, I do believe that the Bridge to the Future, modeled after Market Creek Plaza, provides us with a working model for commercial and residential real-estate management and community development. We were making good progress in our planning and development efforts when the bottom fell out of the market. We now have a comprehensive plan that has been integrated, at least on a preliminary basis, with the economic development plans of the city of Huntington Beach, and we have a vision of what is possible in the future. For me, the words are quite literal: the vision of renewal is enabled and made possible by the Bridge to the Future.

SUMMARY

Once again, the primary role of the Oak View Renewal Partnership is that of being a catalyst. We have worked with our resource partners and brought new partners to Oak View. We are not real estate developers, property managers, or a financial institution. We are an organization that brings those assets together to achieve the vision and mission of the organization.

It is my hope that through an understanding of the housing issues, bringing the resources to the community, and facilitating an interaction between tenants and property owners we may help to provide relief to a difficult situation and move toward our vision of empowerment and renewal.

CHAPTER XII

*Economic And Social
Enterprise—Building A
Sustainable Community*

If we build it, they may come.
—JACK SHAW

INTRODUCTION

As we continue to track the Exhibit II-2, the Community
Environment Loop, Social and Economic Force becomes the force
that drives empowerment and renewal. We may ultimately narrow
the gaps of urban hardship, but economic sustainability will be the
final test of success for our One Square Mile. As I will discuss later
in this chapter, our ability to attract capital to fund commerce will
be key to that sustainability.

Establishing economic freedom, creating jobs, and attracting capital are all required to build communities that are self-sustaining. Our business model or theory of change for community

empowerment and renewal, if it is to be successful, must be self-sustaining and not dependent on public funding, contributions, and grants for its continued survival.

STRUCTURE AND PROCESS
Overarching Strategy—A Fund of Funds

Prior to the "Great Recession" of 2008, the Bridge to the Future, which I introduced in Chapter XI, represented our strategy for attracting capital and creating a balance sheet for the community. We knew we must create an organization that was sustainable beyond raising money every year to meet our operating needs. We knew that our executive director, and indeed our board, would be spending more time raising money than they spent working on the issues of empowerment and renewal. It remains my hope that our business model will be sustainable long term as a result of the creation of social enterprises that will provide our investors with a return on their capital as well as operating funds to achieve our mission.

The fund of funds relates to some combination of social investors who see Oak View and our organization as a model for the future and who are willing to invest in a fund that would help assure that future. Those investors may include program-related Investments (PRI) from foundations, community development financial institutions (CDFI), and wealthy social investors. Iosefa has termed this form of investment as a community foundation model. What he has in mind is the creation of a fund that would support the activities of our community partners.

Social Enterprise Institute and Academy

Around the time the Oak View Renewal Partnership was getting started, a veteran of the social enterprise movement, Dave McDonough, brought to Orange County an organization known as the Social Enterprise Institute. The Institute, sponsored by what was then called the Volunteer Center, brought to Orange County a body of knowledge around the subject of social enterprise and the concept of earned income that had not previously been well established. While there were some examples of nonprofit organizations that earned income while having a charitable mission, those examples were few and far between. Except for Goodwill Industries, the idea that nonprofit organizations having a "for-profit" mission was considered by many to be socially unacceptable. The Social Enterprise Institute changed all of that.

According to Betsy Densmore, president and CEO of the Academies for Social Entrepreneurship, Dave McDonough's initial contributions to the cause of social enterprise spawned a number of initiatives:

- Social Enterprise Leadership Forums, hosted by Dave and Mark VanNess, a local entrepreneur. The forums brought nonprofit executives, including myself, together to explore earned income opportunities.

- Social Enterprise Academy, developed by Andy Horowitz, a local venture capitalist, and Betsy Densmore. The academy integrated its efforts with another local organization, the Tech Coast Angels.

- The Academies for Social Entrepreneurship, founded by Betsy Densmore, playing the role of convener and catalyst, connecting the organizations and people needed to create and finance social enterprises. Betsy has been a real spark igniting the entrepreneurial spirit of the nonprofits in Orange County. According to Betsey, over 90 percent of the sixty Orange County charities that have participated say that the program significantly impacted the way they do business, and 64 percent generated new earned income within a few months.

Social Enterprise Venture Fund

In 2007, all of these initiatives led my wife and me to start what is now known as the Social Enterprise Venture Fund at the Orange County Community Foundation. The Social Enterprise Venture Fund served as an initial source of funds, as well as a framework for attracting additional investments intended to help nonprofits to establish social-enterprise ventures. The Social Enterprise Venture Fund assisted the Oak View Renewal Partnership to create the HB Mercado Certified Farmers Market, which will be discussed later in this chapter.

At the heart of social enterprise is the requirement that a business plan be created, capital raised, and leadership identified. The Social Enterprise Venture Fund was established to achieve those purposes.

The Social Enterprise Venture Fund has provided "seed capital" for several startups having their origins in Oak View:

- The HB Mercado Certified Farmers Market

- e-Smiles, a social-enterprise venture of Healthy Smiles for Kids of Orange County

- Emoción, a promotional products venture of El Viento and the Oak View Renewal Partnership

Our new enterprises are paving the way toward a culture of entrepreneurial innovation within each organization while providing earned income to help sustain the organizations involved.

The Social Enterprise Committee

We have combined the social-enterprise activities of El Viento and OVRP into one committee serving the Oak View Committee. We are most fortunate to have, serving with me as co-chair, Brenda

Glim, a well-known entrepreneur from Huntington Beach and a member of the El Viento board of directors. Brenda has created numerous startup ventures including a promotional-products business that she most generously donated to our organizations and that formed the basis for Emoción. Our committee, which consists of members of both organizations, meets frequently to discuss new ideas and to oversee the creation of business plans for submission to the Social Enterprise Venture Fund.

Leadership Development

Nothing happens without effective leadership. Leaders bring the vision, energy, and enthusiasm to projects without which there would be no innovation. The Oak View Renewal Partnership is very fortunate to have the support of the Orange County Goodwill organization in the implementation of a leadership development course for our residents. The Goodwill course, Future Business Owners, recently completed a twelve-week pilot project for the Oak View Community. The course was intended to develop in our residents the skills necessary to start their own businesses. This program, with funding provided by the Santa Ana Workforce Investment Board, AT&T, and Wells Fargo, is one of many we hope to bring to the community as we try to leverage the basic entrepreneurial culture of our residents. We will be providing courses in the future that emphasize these competencies:

- Financial literacy

- Access to capital through micro-loans

- Development of business plans

It is our intention that the leaders who take part in such initiatives as the Goodwill course will ultimately take responsibility for all of our social-enterprise programs. Those programs, managed by local leaders, will be at the core of our vision of empowerment and renewal.

EXAMPLES OF WHAT IS WORKING
HBMercado Certified Farmers Market

The Oak View Renewal Partnership farmer's market project took nearly four years to get off the ground. From the inception of the concept to opening day, the journey of the first social-enterprise project took many turns:

- The creation of a feasibility study and business plan funded by the Social Enterprise Venture Fund and the Orange County Community Foundation

- Establishing a venue and securing approvals from all parties involved

- Raising capital to cover the first year of operating cash flow

- Selecting and engaging a partner that would operate the market

- Preparation for the launch

- Schedule opening day for May 21, 2011

- Continuous operation—every Saturday

The feasibility study and business-planning activities were the easy part. The most rewarding aspect of the project was the enthusiastic support of the city of Huntington Beach and Huntington Beach Union High School District. Kellee Fritzal, the deputy director of Economic Development, was and is extremely enthusiastic about the project. Kellee paved the way though the complex regulatory and public-hearing processes as well as providing us with the benefit of her farmers-market experience in other communities.

Along with the city, we received tremendous support from Union High School District and from Ocean View High School, the planned location of the market. Led by the former superintendent, Van Riley, the district board, and the newly selected principal, Dan Bryan, a formal partnership was created with the Oak View Renewal Partnership.

Partnerships such as the one we forged with the high school are the essence of social enterprise. No single organization, much less a startup, can go it alone. The HB Mercado Organic Farmers Market partnership was formed with a set of guiding principles that, in turn, formed the basis for a legal agreement:

- Profits, after establishing reserves, would be shared equally.

- Ocean View High School would furnish the space and OVRP would manage the market.

It was as simple as that—a true partnership among trusted parties.

The next major step in the process was the selection of a partner to manage the market on behalf of OVRP. After a thorough search, we selected Vela, an East Los Angeles nonprofit community development organization that also successfully manages farmers markets around the Los Angeles area. Vela, led by executive director Grace Gonzales, project manager Jose Cervantez, and site manager Juan Gonzales, has been a wonderful partner. Vela has brought vendors whose products are in demand by the residents of Oak View as well as greater Huntington Beach, and has proved to be a knowledgeable and experienced partner.

As I write this book, the HBMercado Certified Farmers Market is meeting or exceeding its revenue and profitability expectations. After six months of operation, the startup is on track with similar farmers market operations at this stage in their development. Our challenge now is to encourage the Oak View community residents to spend more of their shopping dollars in our market. Given the dire economic situation in which our families find themselves, this challenge is daunting. We are going to have to work very hard over the next six months to achieve the promise of the venture.

Emoción

The promotional products business, Emoción, was facilitated by Brenda Glim working with the El Viento high school students. Brenda, who owned her own promotional-products business, worked with our students to establish the overall business concept. I sat in on a number of sessions with the students as they designed T-shirts and established a name for their company. The enthusiastic participation of the group was truly exciting. During the first year of operation, a large number of designer T-shirts were sold in addition to special orders for events in Orange County. The business model is sound, and the economics work; we have the operating capability to deliver the product...except we are missing the leadership necessary to take the business to the next level. As I mentioned above, leadership is the critical factor in the development of anything, and in particular, an entrepreneurial startup. It is my hope that the various leadership-development initiatives we have undertaken within OVRP will yield a leader willing and able to move this project forward.

LESSONS LEARNED—WHAT I WOULD DO DIFFERENTLY

Having a good or even great idea is not enough. "If you build it they will come" may actually be paraphrased as "If you *only* build it, they will not come." If I had the opportunity to restart all of the social-enterprise activities that I have fostered within El Viento, Healthy Smiles for Kids of Orange County, and the Oak View Renewal Partnership, I would start with having the leaders in place before I did anything else. Leadership has made all the difference in the world in the success of the Oak View Renewal Partnership. As I mentioned in Chapter IV, we could not have restarted the Oak View Renewal Partnership without having Iosefa on board. But one person can't do everything. The old story that you give a busy person the responsibility for something new only works so far. We must develop leaders at all levels before we can begin to realize the potential of our initiatives.

SUMMARY

The culture of the Oak View community and its residents embodies hard work and a drive to become socially and economically independent. The challenge for our community partners and the Oak View Renewal Partnership is to leverage that culture and to help our residents achieve that independence. Creating meaningful, valued work that fosters pride and dignity is the greatest contribution we may make to our community. Specifically, we must

- attract the capital required for organizational stability and sustainability,

- provide our potential entrepreneurs with the leadership and business management skills they require become successful,

- provide the seed capital and micro-loan financing necessary to start up local enterprises, and

- help to create the markets and stimulate demand for the products and services being offered.

In other words, we must lend a helping hand to incubate the entrepreneurial spirit inherent in the culture of the community. Our social-enterprise efforts are designed to achieve that outcome.

As my Texas friends might say, "We are fixin' to get ready." I feel that, as far as social enterprise is concerned, we are at the starting block. We have some great ideas, we have launched one venture that has promise, but we have a long way to go. We have two major challenges to overcome:

- Leadership
- Culture

I have discussed leadership in some depth here and elsewhere, but I can't overestimate the importance of getting this right. In my view, and based on all of my experiences, it is better not to start a venture if the required leadership is not in place. Poor leadership is not only ineffective; it ruins the opportunity for others who may come along. Precious time, money, and inertia are wasted.

I discussed the role of culture at some length in Chapter V. Culture drives everything. In my opinion, culture defines success or failure of organizations large and small. So it is with communities. We must understand and deal with the culture of the community if change is to take place. Using social enterprise as a vehicle for creating a sustainable community only works if the community is invested in the enterprise or initiative. We are learning that such investments are made one household at a time. Sitting across the kitchen table discussing the importance of an initiative and getting a personal commitment to that initiative is the only way to leverage the culture of the community to achieve change.

CHAPTER XIII

Scaling Up—Exporting The Model

Give me a lever long enough, and single-handed, I can move the world.

—ARCHIMEDES

INTRODUCTION

I was recently asked what it would take to transfer our pilot organization to other communities. Of course, one of the goals of the Oak View Renewal Partnership is just that: "to change the world, one community at a time." The question really brought about a twofold response. First, the Oak View Renewal Partnership itself must be successful and sustainable. If we are to prove the case, we must first "scale up" OVRP. Second, within our business model or theory of change, there are at least five conditions that I believe are necessary not only to transfer the concept, but to assure the viability of OVRP itself:

1. Leadership—as I have stressed all along, nothing gets done without visionary, purposeful leaders.

2. Focus—any community-renewal effort must be focused on a manageable, demographically uniform market and customers. Incorporated in this focus, as is the case with any market segment, goes a deep understanding of the difference between, needs, wants, and expectations.

3. Outcomes measurement—results that are objective, measurable, and indicative of the changes required are essential to achieving the mission of the organization.

4. Accountability—the leaders and the board must take responsibility for changing the condition of the community.

5. Capital—community empowerment and renewal takes time and money. OVRP must have a strong balance sheet if it is to survive, and any organization hoping to embark on a similar path must be strongly capitalized to endue for the long journey of empowerment and renewal.

I believe that the first four conditions are present in the Oak View Renewal Partnership; however, the fifth condition, capital, is not present. There may be additional conditions, but I know firsthand that in the absence of the above factors, nothing will happen.

In short, scaling up, repeatability, and sustainability begin at home. The Oak View Renewal Partnership will only serve as a model for other communities if it, as a pilot organization, is itself sustainable.

STRUCTURE AND PROCESS
Overarching Strategy
The Oak View Renewal Partnership is a business. Our business model or theory of change is, in my opinion, a prerequisite for any

organization to consider when attempting to scale up or transfer the concept of OVRP to another community. Most importantly, we are not in the business of delivering social-service programs, however defined. We are a catalyst for change in our One Square Mile community. This distinction is critical to lessons of OVRP, as those lessons apply to other communities. As I discussed in Chapter II, "A Business Model for Community Empowerment and Renewal," there are several important concepts that lie beneath the surface of OVRP:

- Systems thinking—the idea of cause and effect, feedback, and learning. That is, we must understand the intended and unintended consequences of our actions. We must understand that everything is connected. This connectivity is the reason why individual programs do not have the desired impact. As I have previously indicated, we have to work on everything at the same time.

- The Service Value Chain. The activities that link our markets, customers, providers, and funders must be closely aligned in order to provide the focus required to serve our market and customers.

- The Community Wellness Index (CWI), which tracks our performance in narrowing the gaps between our One Square Mile and the remainder of Orange County.

In my view these elements of the business model differentiate what we are trying to do in Oak View with other, more traditional community development initiatives. I believe that our business model is working in Oak View, and according to one individual whom I interviewed, "OVRP has taken Oak View to an entirely new level."

"Deep Pockets"

As we observe and learn from other "place-based" initiatives, in particular the Harlem Children's Zone, Market Creek Plaza, and Building Healthy Communities, each organization has a common thread that enables it to stay the course over the long run: *capital*. The Harlem Children's Zone has the benefit of a strong backing from Wall Street investors, Market Creek Plaza received its initial funding from the Jacobs Family Foundation, and Building Healthy Communities has received its funding from the California Endowment.

While the Oak View Renewal Partnership has benefitted enormously from its initial funders, we are by no means assured of sustainability without attracting funds beyond our operating budget. In other words, we need deep pockets if we are to survive and provide a model for other communities. Our basic strategy for scaling up must include a search for capital.

"Flood the Zone"

David Brooks, the renowned *New York Times* columnist, penned a most thoughtful piece on February 7, 2012, entitled "Flood the Zone." I am going to quote an excerpt that I feel sums up the case for dealing with poverty at a community level, and that, I feel, supports our case for systems thinking as we scale up the concept of OVRP including to other sites.

> The list of factors that contribute to poverty could go on and on, and the interactions between them are infinite. Therefore, there is no single magic lever to pull to significantly reduce poverty. The only thing to do is change the whole ecosystem.
>
> If poverty is a complex system of negative feedback loops, then you have to create an equally complex and diverse set of positive loops. You have to flood the zone with as many good programs as you can find and fund and hope that somehow they will interact and reinforce each other community by community, neighborhood by neighborhood.

The column goes on to provide important examples, but suffice it to say Exhibit II-2, The Community Environment, is the positive feedback loop articulated in Mr. Brooks's column.

Our board member Scott Smith, who has been working in Oak View for a long time, summarizes his thoughts that accentuate the positive about the future of Oak View:

> *Oak View is a uniquely American neighborhood, full of families seeking to make a better life for their children. This One Square Mile shows the world that with a few tools and a sense of pride, a community can accomplish just about anything.*

EXAMPLES OF WHAT IS WORKING
Market Creek Plaza

I have referred to Market Creek Plaza a number of times during my journey. I was referred to the San Diego organization in 2005 by Armando de la Libertad while he was still with Wells Fargo Bank. I was looking for a community-based model to test my ideas for Oak View and to see if any other organizations where doing what we were considering. A group of us visited Market Creek Plaza and met with Roque Barros, the director of community relations. Roque and his colleagues were very generous with their time and with the experiences of the Jacobs Family Foundation. Roque also visited Oak View and met with our advisory board. Since 2005, my colleagues and I have traveled to Market Creek Plaza many times and have witnessed the growth and success of the community. During our visits to Market Creek Plaza, we took away several important lessons, including

- the need to work on everything at once,
- the process of empowerment as a "bottoms up" activity centered around community organizing,

- the realization that some efforts will fail and have to be started anew, and

- the fact that the process of renewal takes a lot of time and money.

It is not my intent to tell the story of Market Creek Plaza except to relate the importance of the work of the Jacobs Family Foundation in the development of a very successful place-based community-development model. We have tried to implement many of the lessons of Market Creek without having the scale or the resources that may be ultimately required for the renewal of our One Square Mile

Building Healthy Communities

The California Endowment (TCE) played a major role in the development of Market Creek Plaza and in the startup of the Oak View Renewal Partnership. Greg Hall and Steve Eldred, program officers, have provided invaluable counsel in our community development efforts as well as significant financial support of Healthy Smiles for Kids of Orange County. We have also learned a great deal from a place-based initiative, Building Healthy Communities, sponsored by TCE in Santa Ana, California.

Greg Hall and his colleagues have engaged in a grass roots community development effort that includes a Promotores model implemented though the Latino Health Access organization, also in Santa Ana. TCE has scaled up Latino Health Access to provide a wide variety of services to a specific geographic area of Santa Ana. As I pointed out above, TCE has committed significant capital to the Building Healthy Communities initiative in their efforts to leverage the experience of a smaller organization.

LESSONS LEARNED—WHAT I SHOULD HAVE DONE DIFFERENTLY

In 2003, the concept of place-based community empowerment and renewal was new, at least to me. It took a trip to Market Creek Plaza for me to discover that such models existed. Of course, I recognized the tremendous benefit the Jacobs Family Foundation capital provided. Indeed, I felt that we would attract investors once the business model of OVRP became more widely established. I think that is still the case, except now I know for certain how capital-intensive such development efforts really are, and that we must create a balance sheet as well as an annual profit-and-loss statement.

In short, I don't think there is much I would or could have done differently, except now as we think about scaling up and making our business model and pilot project transferrable to other communities, the role of capital cannot be overemphasized. We simply cannot take the theory of change, move it to another "place," and expect it to take root without the availability of significant financial support. Annual grants and other contributions are necessary but not sufficient conditions for success.

SUMMARY

We can do this!

I really believe that our vision of empowerment and renewal will become a reality. I really believe that the American Dream is available to the residents of the Oak View community. To paraphrase the song from the Broadway hit *New York, New York,* if we can't do it here, we can't do it anywhere. All of the stars and planets are aligned to enable us to move from fear to trust. We just have to do it!

Zayda Garcia has put this dream into a different context:

OVRP has been like a "revolution of hope and dreams" in the Oak View community. A "movement" of hope for a brighter future for the children and young adults of the Oak View community was ignited by El Viento. OVRP provided the fuel necessary for that ignition to begin actualizing the entire Oak View community's hopes and dreams for a brighter future. We dreamed of a cleaner community, we dreamed of a soccer league for a families, we dreamed of a farmers market to bring together all of Huntington Beach. We dreamed, and created a road map to make our dreams come true, and they have! We are still dreaming and are united in our "revolution to make the rest of our hopes and dreams come true." We still want better housing conditions, educational attainment, and a safer community.

What an inspiring message from someone who has herself lived the "dream."

In Closing

As I wrap up this journal and my journey, I cannot help but communicate what a wonderful trip this has been. A new generation of leaders is taking over El Viento, Healthy Smiles, and soon, OVRP; and that is as it should be. I have high hopes and great expectations for the vision and mission of our One Square Mile. I know, based on the progress of the past fifteen years, our community will become empowered and renewed. I know the barriers of fear will be replaced with pathways to empowerment and choice. I am very grateful to all who have taken this trip with me, for without every one of you, we would not be where we are. As I said in the preface to this journal, we are at the end of the beginning.

Thank you!

APPENDIX 1

Briefing for Congressman Chris Cox
DECEMBER 4, 2003

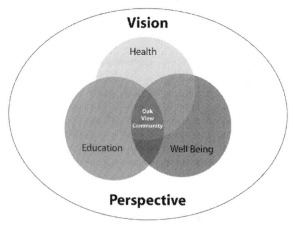

Golden West College / El Viento Foundation

Oak View 2010 Project

A Proposal for Community Renewal

A Proposal to Create a Model Community

Assessment of the Situation

The Oak View district of Huntington Beach is a one square mile community:

- 1,500 families in a densely populated, multi-family residential neighborhood

- 7,500 individuals

- 99+% Hispanic or Latino

- Median age of the population is 20-26 years

Considerable Federal and city resources have been directed to the Oak View community, including:

- HUD Grants of over $1 million per year for the past five years

- Police and public services

Conclusion

Notwithstanding the resources committed and attention paid to the community, the education, health and other characteristics of well-being have not kept pace with the remainder of the Huntington Beach community.

- All students perform below grade level in all subjects

- Pediatric oral health issues have reached epidemic proportions

- Health care needs are met by either a community clinic or local emergency rooms

- 100% of the individual population is below poverty level

- Population density is 7,500 per square mile, at least twice the average for Huntington Beach

- Average household size is six, also twice the size of Huntington Beach

El Viento has established a model program for community development which is working.

- The average GPA is above the average for Huntington Beach

- "Triggered" Orange County oral health initiative

- Provides a catalyst for family development

Overarching Strategy

Using the resources of Golden West College and the El Viento Model, establish model program for community development which will raise the average of:

- Health

- Education

- Well-Being

For the entire community and which will be capable of being replicated across other similar communities.

Approach

Using a combination of private and public sector resources, establish specific health, education and well-being programs designed to change the condition of the families and children of the Oak View community.

APPENDEX 11

Oak View Strategic Plan

JUNE, 2006

INTRODUCTION

Oak View is an approximately one square mile community within the city of Huntington Beach. The Oak View Renewal Partnership is a non-profit corporation established to empower the Oak View Community.

The mission of the Oak View Renewal Partnership is to narrow the cultural, social, educational and economic gap between the Oak View Community and the remainder of Huntington Beach and to serve as a model for community development.

The Planning Studio at UC Irvine's Department of Policy, Planning and Design was requested by the Oak View Renewal Partnership to develop a strategic plan to support the renewal and economic development strategies for the community.

In order to complete this report the Planning Studio students divided into four teams: 1) Community Needs; 2) Design; 3) Gateway Parcel Opportunities and

4) Implementation Strategies. Although the students worked at times separately with their teams, the overall Strategic Plan is a product of the entire Studio Class.

This report represents the first step in a renewal process that empowers the residents of the Oak View Community.

UNIVERSITY OF CALIFORNIA, IRVINE
CLASS OF 2006

Jared Eskenazi

Jason Ficht

Ryan Graham

Jarett Jensen

Suzy Kim

Natalia Komar

David Mason

Waen Messner

Lan Nguyen

Jessica Nixon

Justin Partridge

Elizabeth Pettis

Michael Powe

Travis Seawards

Hilary Smith

Sidney Stone

Lesley Whittaker

Kimberly Wong

COMMUNITY ASSESSMENT

INTRODUCTION

The Community Assessment Team spent three months getting to know the Oak View Community, its residents, and those involved with the community. Through various data collection methods, we have gathered valuable data and useful information that we hope are beneficial to the community and the Oak View Renewal Partnership Board. Our goal was to assess community needs and assets that include current living conditions, safety concerns, accessibility, economic feasibility, amenities, and future visions for the community.

This report discusses the methods used to obtain the data and also provides our analysis of the gathered information. The acquired data and findings are divided into three categories: (I) What the data tells us; and (II) What the people told us; and (III) Strengths, Weaknesses, Opportunities & Threats (SWOT). The first category examines demographic assessments, obtained from the U.S. Census Bureau. The second category evaluates information gathered from residents and individuals involved in the community. Lastly, the third category analyzes specifics about the community's strengths, weaknesses, opportunities, and threats (SWOT).

We would like to thank Britta Strother, Oak View Property Owners Association, City of Huntington Beach Parks and Recreation, Oak View Task Force Team, YMCA, Get Your Groove On, El Viento Youth and Parents, Oak View Community Resource Center, Huntington Beach Police Department, Huntington Beach Library, Trinity Properties, Madres Unidas, and Rainbow Disposal for their assistance in making this report possible. Because of their help, we were able to learn more about Oak View and obtain critical information for this report. Their tremendous support and guidance were greatly needed and much appreciated. Thank you.

METHODS

We used both direct and indirect methods to gather data and information on Oak View. Our methods included a survey and informal interviews based on a questionnaire, attending community meetings, participating in community events and activities, and transferring data from the U.S. Census Bureau and the Oak View 2010 Project Report. The primary methods used were informal interviews and surveying based on the questionnaire.

We conducted interviews with various groups in the Oak View Community. These interviews were generally informal and only a few of our group members participated in each meeting, in an effort to create a more personal and friendly environment for our participants. During our interviews we asked a series of

questions from the questionnaire we designed (see Appendix A). In addition to personal interviews, we passed out question-naires for residents and stakeholders to complete.

Data from the Oak View 2010 Project Report and the U.S. Census Bureau provided insight on the demographics of the area while interviews provided community perspectives on programs and services, physical neighborhood conditions, safety, mobility, and economic opportunities.

I. WHAT THE DATA TELLS US

Demographic characteristics provide information on the composition of the Oak View community. Although demographic data helps one understand the composition of the community, it is important to note that demographic data can be misleading, possibly resulting in stereotyping the community and the individuals within the community. Oak View's demographic information in this section is taken from the 2000 United States Census. The census data provides a snapshot of the characteristics of the community and provides useful information for our analysis. However, it can also be flawed due to low response rates in neighborhoods with a preponderance of immigrants and high proportions of non-English speaking residents.

Oak View is located within two (2) census block groups, block 994.02 groups 3 and 4 (U.S. Census, accessed May 12, 2006). The community is comprised of approximately 6,000 residents, with 86% of the community identified as Latino, and only 13% of households have a member (14 years of age or older) who speaks English without difficulty. In addition, 63% of the community is of foreign birth and 57% are not United States citizens, which means of the 63% foreign born only 10% have become United States citizens (U.S. Census, accessed May 12, 2006). This low naturalization rate compared to the 38% in Orange County overall, and 40% United States average may be an indicator of barriers to naturalization within the community (U.S. Census, accessed May 12, 2006).

The Oak View community is comprised of a young population in comparison to the surrounding city. The median age of Oak View is 23 in comparison to the Huntington Beach median age of 36 years old (U.S. Census, accessed May 12, 2006). The young age of the community influences the demand for the types of services such as schools, youth sports groups, and daycare services. In Oak View, only 25% of community members aged 25 years and older have a high school diploma, in comparison to the surrounding Huntington Beach community which exceeds the United States average of 80% WS. Census, accessed May 12, 2006). This low educational attainment in the community demonstrates a very large educational gap between Oak View and the rest of Huntington Beach.

The community has an average family size of 5.5 members and a median family income of $32,000. In comparison, Huntington Beach as a whole earns a median family income of $74,000 with an average family size of 3 members (U.S. Census, accessed May 12, 2006). The difference in median incomes exemplifies the need to address the economic gap between Oak View and its neighbors. The low median income is also very alarming considering the median family income of Oak View falls well below the county's average level needed to rent a one-bedroom apartment and maintain an acceptable quality of life. The family size, median family income and county median rent would suggest that this community is prone to overcrowding. This community is made of 97% renters making them very sensitive to fluctuations in the housing market.

II. WHAT THE PEOPLE TOLD US: FINDINGS FROM THE OAK VIEW COMMUNITY ASSESSMENT SURVEY

In order to understand the community, semi-structured and informal interviews in conjunction with a survey were conducted with youth and adult residents, city agencies, service providers, and members of the business community. The purpose of the interviews was to discuss current resources and needs in the area. Interviews were conducted with the following groups: Oak View Property Owners Association, City of Huntington Beach Parks and Recreation, Task Force, YMCA, Get Your Groove On, El Viento Youth and Parents, and Huntington Beach Police Department, Trinity Properties, Madres Unidas, and Rainbow Disposal.

Findings

This section reveals the findings from the Oak View Community Assessment Questionnaire (see Appendix A for the questionnaire sample). The findings are organized into three (3) themes as follows: social themes, physical environment themes, and interesting findings. The social themes consist of a group of concerns that could be overcome through the implementation of social programs and services. The physical environment themes are concerns pertaining to infrastructure and could be addressed through the private sector and local, regional and national government initiatives. A set of interesting findings is included to give insight on other important issues facing the community.

Social Themes:

- *Connecting people with services:* While there are many programs and services for children under the age of 10, residents expressed little knowledge of programs for people outside of this age group. However, service providers indicated that programs and services are plentiful for all age groups but are underutilized. In order to provide additional outreach to the community and educate them of the programs and services available, service providers must conduct more outreach and publicity. In addition, service groups should consider providing additional programs that residents would participate in such as gang and drug prevention programs.

- *Overcrowding:* Interviewees reported that the occupancy rate ranges between 2 to 10 people in a one-bedroom apartment. It is common for families to rent out floor space to a stranger or relative, in order to pay rent which ranges from a total of $975-$1,200. Some small property owners recognize overcrowding as an issue that can contribute to the deterioration of the property, resulting from overuse of an apartment. However, overcrowding is difficult to manage because these owners rarely visit their properties in Oak View to monitor the problem. Owners are also hesitant to evict good tenants who need to sublet space in the apartment to pay rent.

- *Day laborers:* There tends to be daily congregation of day laborers on Slater Avenue, in hopes of finding employment for the day. During April and May 2006, the Huntington Beach Police Department (HBPD) encouraged workers to seek employment at the neighboring work center, located on Gothard Street, just south of Slater Avenue. So far, day laborers have complied, but they do not often commit to stay at the center until noon (the center's closing time) because there is a limited supply of jobs. Despite the encouragement of potential employers by HBPD and center staff to hire laborers through the work center, some contractors are hesitant to use the center because of the administrative process. The center requires them to document the number of times they employ day laborers. Eliminating the congregation of workers on Slater Avenue has several positive aspects for the area. First, Trinity Properties reports that more people are visiting rental properties. Secondly, parents and young women in the community welcome the move as the unemployed men gawk and whistle at girls and women walking along Slater Avenue.

- *Confused community identity:* The study area for this report is called Oak View but outsiders refer to it as Slater Slums. The residents of Oak View do not identify their community as Oak View or a special enclave, but rather as Huntington Beach. The residents feel that placing a name on the community may have a positive effect on the community as a whole. Although the community name is not well identified, there are signs of strong community relationships due to familial and friendship ties.

- *Graffiti:* This is a continual challenge for residents and property owners and managers. Community groups are nervous about removing the graffiti because they fear retaliation from gangs, and property owners feel defeated due to the consistent appearance of graffiti on their property. While property owners fight the graffiti battle on a weekly basis, the graffiti often reappears immediately after its removal.

Physical Themes:

- *Safe Places:* The Community Resource Center and Oak View Elementary School are seen as the safest places to be during the day and evening. Concerns regarding safety revolve around the presence of gangs, drug dealers, and vandalism, especially in the evening hours. In addition, respondents expressed concerns over slow police responses and insufficient patrol.

- *Need for Latino market:* Residents expressed that there is a need for a Latino supermarket. Currently, residents purchase food from vending trucks and local grocery stores that do not always carry cultural goods. Some residents go to Northgate Supermarkets in Santa Ana and receive a free ride back to Oak View if they purchase more than $50 of goods.

- *Insufficient lighting:* Respondents noted that there is insufficient lighting throughout the community, specifically in the alleys between the school and apartments and on Nichols Street.

- *Traffic problems:* These problems include speeding and insufficient parking both on an off the street. Oak View residents expressed concerns about illegal parking such as comer and double parking. Illegal parking can reduce the street circulation and increase the number of blind spots. In addition, speeding occurs at entryways of the communities. The City's Code Enforcement and Police Department teams have not provided sufficient patrol to reduce illegal parking. In addition, traffic calming devices (e.g. speed bumps) may be needed to reduce speeds though the neighborhood and to improve traffic safety.

- *Trash overload:* There is an abundance of trash around the neighborhood. It is especially problematic around vendor trucks and trash bins. Trash on the streets is not only an eye sore but also a health problem, as respondents reported rodent problems.

Interesting findings:

- *Loan programs are not viable options for property owners:* When property owners were asked if they would participate in a loan program to rehabilitate rental units, they explained that they were not interested. Many property owners did not want to be constrained to government regulations and reporting requirements required by loan programs because they have a minimal number of rental units. Loan programs typically require rent control, which financially constrains new property owners from meeting their high mortgages. In addition, rent control reduces the incentive to reinvest in a property.

- *Improvement of health services:* Community members communicated the limited level of health services available to the community in addition to the limited amount of staff at the neighboring Huntington Beach medical clinic. Medical and dental services need to be improved and increased.

- *High mobility to access goods and services:* Residents reported that goods and services are accessible through waking, biking, and public transportation.

III. STRENGTHS WEAKNESSESS OPPORTUNITIES THREATS (SWOT) ANALYSIS:

The information gathered from group interviews, surveys, and observations were analyzed by conducting a SWOT analysis. The SWOT (strengths, weaknesses, opportunities, and threats) analysis is a tool for auditing an organization and its environment. It can be the first stage of redeveloping and revitalizing a community, and is often used to create a focus on key issues in the community.

Strengths:

The large turn-out for meetings, community events and interviews is a good indication that residents and those who work in the community are interested and committed to improving and supporting the revitalization of Oak View. The consistent responses received from the interviews can assist service providers in more easily identifying problems and potential solutions in the Oak View community. Residents benefit from the wealth of services provided by the, the Oak View Elementary School, the City of Huntington Beach, the Oak View Resource Center, and other community service providers.

Weaknesses:

The high proportion of undocumented persons is a concern for many reasons. These include the possibility that a lack of citizenship or legal documentation may prevent immigrants from seeking help when needed, and that federal funds may also be limited to citizens. Other weaknesses include low income, low educational attainment, residential overcrowding and limited access to community services for adolescents and adults. For many Oak View residents, an inability to speak English can hamper their interactions and opportunities in the U.S.

Opportunities:

Oak View's location in a City redevelopment area makes the community eligible to utilize City economic development tools and funding. These tools can help to revitalize the physical and economic status of the neighborhood. In addition, the Oak View community is potentially eligible for federal community development aid due to its employment status. Physical opportunities include currently vacant parcels that may be available for redevelopment in the future, which can provide economic and/or social growth within the community. The greatest opportunity is the wealth of information and manpower within the community and from those outside who are, or may be interested in supporting the community.

Threats:

From our observations there is a lack of local government support. Although the City has long-range redevelopment plans for the area targeting revitalization of a retail center and low income housing units, these plans do not specifically directly apply to the Oak View community. The stigma of being referred to as the "Slater Slums" may dissuade investors from investing in the area. Lastly, residents have limited access to traditional financial opportunities such as obtaining loans to purchase a home.

Conclusion

In order to provide recommendations to redevelop the community it was necessary to assess the community's needs and assets that include current living conditions, safety concerns, accessibility, economic feasibility, amenities, and future vision for the community. The receptiveness of the community members during the interviews to articulate their concerns and needs is an indication of the interest and knowledge for change to improve the community. The responses provided from the community helps provide recommendations to improve the physical, social, and other aspects of the community that can be incorporated through expanding services and programs, improvements throughout the community, and development of key parcels in Oak View.

COMMUNITY DESIGN

There are many design elements that give a community a sense of place, a feeling of safety and an opportunity for community integration. There is a concern, however, that many of these elements are missing from Oak View. Some of the problems found in Oak View include insufficient lighting, speeding along the streets, illegal parking, inconsistent signage, under-utilized open parcels and overcrowded alleyways. Following is a description of five specific recommendations to enhance the community and improve the safety of its residents. Suggestions include creating streetlight banners, improving the security lighting, utilizing open parcels, traffic solutions, and enhancing the alleyways.

Streetlight Banners

One way to enhance the sense of identity of the region near the Oak View School is with banners on the streetlights. This system is often used by unique city districts, such as downtowns or historic regions, to provide notice of a location's special status to the public.

These banners can also hearld civic events, such as an exhibit at a local cultural center. No matter the use, light pole banners can serve as an outlet for community artistic and cultural expression and pride.

Several different types of banners are available (from, and any banner program would have to pass design review at the City of Huntington Beach's Planning Department. Most banner bracket systems, the metal hardware used to attach the banner to the street-light, can withstand sustained winds of 60-70 mph.

For a single banner of 30 inches, the brackets cost $70, and for a double banner of 30 inches the brackets cost $90. If this cost were funded by the Renewal Partnership or if non-profit organizations or the City of Huntington Beach helped to pay for these banners, the economic impact would be minimal. For some events, banners are hung across city streets. These would likely not be used in the Oak View region.

The community leaders should be very receptive to the idea of streetlight banners but one unresolved question is the name of the community. Still, these banners can be rotated to celebrate the seasons, holidays, or local events. The greatest benefit of the streetlight banners would be to connect Oak View to the rest of Huntington Beach.

Oak View Lighting

Lighting is an important concern in the Oak View community. While the city of Huntington Beach has introduced new street lighting elements in recent years, the current situation suggests this coverage is inadequate. Adequate coverage of lighting in residential neighborhoods is important for resident safety, mobility and sense of control. Some areas of Oak View are better lit than others. Investment in traditional street light fixtures is expensive, but there are effective and cost efficient ways the problem can be addressed by community members and property owners.

A lack of outdoor lighting is strongly related to perceptions of danger and disorder (Fisher and Nasar, 1992) especially among women (Nasar and Smith, 1997; Day, 1999). Dark areas can potentially harbor thieves or assailants and can obscure pedestrians from passing motorists. This can lead to diminished travel after dark, atrophic neighborhood and community ties among residents and a growing sense of fear and entrapment at night. In the Community Assessment Team's survey of residents, only 5 out of 20 respondents gave a favorable review of the lighting in their neighborhood. A number of them responded that the lighting situation was "very bad" or that there was "very little light."

The Community Design Team toured the Oak View neighborhood at night to observe the functioning of street lights and which areas seemed to be the darkest. Well-lit areas included the northern sections of Oak View, north of the elementary school along Oak Street and east along Cypress Street and Sycamore Avenue. Areas of less light coverage included the southern portion of the neighborhood, along Slater Avenue and along Queens Lane, (cited by some survey respondents as dangerous) Koledo Drive and Mandrell Drive. Street lights on Koledo provided little lighting; while Mandrell Drive appeared to suffer from inadequate street light coverage as do the and areas of Dairyview Circle and portions of Nichols Street. Residents also indicated that the alley passage beginning at the end of Oak Street and leading between the apartment garages and the elementary school is dangerous and poorly lit at night.

There are simple and relatively inexpensive solutions to this problem. Homes along Cypress Avenue and apartment buildings along its intersection with Oak Street are equipped with exterior security lighting fixtures above the garage entries. These fixtures effectively illuminate the front elevation of the building as well as the yard and adjacent sidewalk areas. These can be purchased and installed by property managers, and will contribute greatly to resident safety and property value stability.

Oak View Opportunity Parcels
There are several vacant parcels located within the Oak View community. The Community Design Team identified three vacant parcels located on Cypress Avenue, which, if utilized strategically, would add to the vitality of Cypress Avenue and serve as a connection

between Oak View and Huntington Beach via Beach Boulevard. Two of the vacant parcels are currently zoned as residential lots and are situated between existing homes. The third parcel is located on the northwest corner of Cypress Avenue and Elm Street. The current zoning for the lot is commercial.

The Community Design Team recommends the use of the commercially zoned lot as a site for a weekly Farmer's Market or a type of vendor's market. Operating a Farmer's Market within Oak View would bring commerce into the community, provide job opportunities for community members, and bring other members of Huntington Beach into Oak View, helping to familiarize with them with the Oak View community. Having a weekly community market will also be a community activity that can encourage participation and result in strengthening relationships and community identity.

The two residential parcels are located between existing homes and activity on these two parcels may be more difficult to have approved, however their immediate location to residents make them ideal parcels to have available to the community as open space. Providing seating, picnic tables, shaded areas, and a play area for children would transform these vacant lots into a social place or a quiet place of relaxation. Having a common land available to the neighborhood allows residents to feel welcome and comfortable outside of their own home and territory. It allows them to feel connected to the greater social community (Alexander et al, 1977).

The Community Assessment Team's survey of Oak View residents revealed that one of the social concerns of Oak View is the desire for more activities, programs, and services within the community. The Community Assessment Team also observed a lack of cohesion between community members. There was little acquaintance with other residents who did not live near each other. Creating a Farmer's Market as well as neighborhood common grounds within Oak View will provide venues and programs for social meetings to take place and will encourage communication between those who participate.

There are other possibilities of uses on these vacant parcels that could fulfill the needs of Oak View members. The Community Design Team encourages residents to consider their needs and mobilize plans that will create social opportunities and allow residents to feel comfortable in the space.

Oak View Traffic

Many of the residents feel traffic patterns in the Oak View community are problematic. It has been observed that some people travel too fast through the intersections creating an unsafe environment for pedestrians and children playing around the streets. The strategic placement of stop signs would help reduce vehicle speed along these streets. The intersection of Sycamore and Ash, for example has a two-way stop sign on each side of Ash Street. Making this into a four-way stop sign would reduce the risk of traffic accidents in this intersection. The intersection of Mandrell Drive and Koledo Lane is a T-shaped intersection. Oftentimes there are children playing or people standing along Mandrell Drive. Many residents have indicated a need for a stop sign on Koledo Lane since it runs into Mandrell Drive.

This can be confusing to residents and visitors and dangerous for children who may be playing in the alleys assuming traffic will only come in one direction. There needs to be an assessment of the signs throughout the community and determine whether they are correctly placed and effective. This is to ensure that traffic is directed in an efficient manner and does not pose any risk to pedestrians or other drivers.

The Oak View community is very densely populated. There is not enough garage or covered parking for the dwelling units. A good number of the residents end up parking on the street. As parking along the street fills up, many end up parking right up to the intersection. When cars stop at the intersection, their visibility is reduced by cars parked at the corners. Accidents are more likely to occur under these circumstances. One suggestion is to paint the curb corners red to deter people from parking in these areas. This will also create a safer environment for pedestrians. Those who continue to park along the painted curbs should be ticketed to ensure compliance. If this area is not policed, people will continue to park in these areas that should be kept clear for pedestrian safety.

Alleyway Improvements

During visits to the Oak View community, the Community Design Team frequently saw neighbors interacting socially in alleyways behind residential units. Gathering around an automobile under repair or standing outside an open window listening to music, Oak View residents seem to use the alleyways both as a functional and social space. This was somewhat unexpected. Traditionally, the design of residential areas facilitates interaction in front of homes in yards or on doorsteps. The Community Design Team strives to improve upon the physical design of the neighborhood in efforts to facilitate the residents' current way of life rather than imposing an external culture or way of living.

In observations, it seemed as though some physical characteristics of the alleyways were problematic for such social interaction, however. For instance, small trash dumpsters are scattered throughout the alleys. Obviously, the dumpsters are associated with severely unpleasant odors. The Team noticed that these dumpsters often had wheels on them. While the mobility of the dumpsters may be useful, larger, more fixed enclosures might improve opportunities for social interaction. If these dumpsters and their associated odors were contained to certain parts of the alley, neighbors might interact more in a more pleasant environment, and such interaction could lead to a greater sense of community and connectedness.

The presence of parked cars also has implications for the use of alleys as social spaces (see photo below). As mentioned above, cars and trucks sometimes inadvertently serve as social gathering points. Neighbors work together repairing their vehicles. However, it is possible that the presence of automobiles also has a negative effect on the social use of the alleyways. The vehicles obstruct views across the alley. This could be a safety issue as well. Drivers of cars traveling the alleyways may not be able to see children as a result of the parked automobiles. However, parking is limited in Oak View, so any change to the availability of parking should be carefully considered and discussed with community residents. Still, centralization of parking could improve visibility, bringing improved safety and the possibility of further interaction among neighbors.

While the alleys are apparently popular social gathering spaces, some other changes could make a powerful positive impact on their social function. For example, the alleys currently do not have any apparent amenities for hanging out with neighbors or friends. The addition of seating, green space, and/or human scale lighting might be beneficial. The Oak View Renewal Partnership should work with local residents and property owners to determine if such amenities would be desirable. Currently, people simply lean against garages or sit on the hoods of cars as they chat. This may be sufficient for the wishes of the community residents, so design interventions should not occur without prior discussion to the possible future users.

Works Cited:

Alexander, C., Ishikawa, S., Silverstein, M., Jacobson, M., Fiksdahl-King, I., Angel, S. (1977). A *Pattern Language*. NY: Oxford University Press.

Day, K. (2000). Strangers in the night? Women's fear of sexual assault on urban college campuses. *Journal of Architectural and Planning Research*, 16 (4), 289-312.

Fisher, B. & Nasar, J.L. (1992). Fear of crime in relation to three exterior site features: Prospect, refuge and escape. *Environment and Behavior,* 24, 35-62

Nasar, J. L.; Jones, K. (1997). Landscapes of Fear and Stress *Environment and Behavior,* vol. 29, no. 3, pp. 291-323.

GATEWAY PARCEL OPPORTUNITIES

The Vision

The Gateway Parcel Redevelopment Team envisions a vibrant, landmark destination that serves as a gateway to the Oak View community. Our redevelopment plan is ambitious and contains strong design elements that illustrate our grand vision for the site. Our group calls this empty piece the Gateway Parcel and that name really defines and illustrates the basis of how we brainstormed and created our ideas for this parcel. We also saw this part of Oak View as having the potential for not only being a Community Gateway, but also a way to give the community an identity, a focal point, and a community gathering space. With the Gateway Parcel Redevelopment Plan, we are making a statement - that the Oak View community deserves socially and economically viable institutions for the betterment and prosperity of the neighborhood's residents.

The Gateway Parcel Redevelopment Plan contains three separate designs. We used the information presented by the Assessment Team, as well as information compiled by taking several visits in the community, to come up with the three alternatives. These alternatives all share three common design elements: an Income

Generating Component, a Community Center (whether as a supplement to existing facilities or as a replacement facility), and Park/Recreation facilities or open green space. The difference in each design is a matter of degree of importance placed on each of these three elements. We designed all of these models with attention and sensitivity to the existing residents and land uses. We also understand that none of these alternatives will necessarily be built exactly as they appear in our illustration.

Purpose of Redevelopment Plan

The intent of this redevelopment plan is to re-design and improve the Gateway Parcel to maximize the site's potential for current and future users, and to meet the economic and social needs of the Oak View community.

Project Objectives

This Gateway Redevelopment Plan uses the following objectives to execute specific land use needs to create a visionary district:

1. Sense of Place

- Create socially and economically viable institutions within the Oak View community, utilizing smart growth and sustainable practices, and establishing a visionary sense of place.

- Improve the image of the Oak View community by providing culturally and ethnically sensitive destination points.

- Create a distinct district by utilizing identifiable signage, streetscaping, murals, and other design strategies.

2. Balance of Land Uses

- Incorporate much-needed community space with new and improved community center facilities

- Provide several economic opportunities through retail, office and training facilities to promote economic prosperity for Oak View residents.

- Provide green space and both active and passive recreational opportunities.

3. Build Economic Value

- Create micro-enterprise and entrepreneurial opportunities for Oak View residents.

- Provide job training and business skill opportunities and facilities

- Create an income-generating opportunity through tax-increment financing for the Oak View community

- Create an income-generating opportunity through tax-increment financing for the Oak View community

Gateway Parcel Redevelopment Plan—Three Alternatives

CONCEPT A: MERCADO, COMMUNITY CENTER, AND COMMUNITY GARDEN

Concept A

The focal points of Concept A are an indoor/outdoor Mercado or marketplace, a community center and a community garden. The Mercado is designed to accomplish several different goals. First, we envision the Mercado as a huge community and cultural amenity that not only honors the Hispanic heritage of the neighborhood, but can also be an institution that gives Oak View a positive identity and provides a strong community focus.

The Mercado concept is simple yet has been effective in so many other Latino communities. Rather then your typical retail strip center, vendors rent out (or win) spaces in a central market-place to sell a variety of goods, most typically fruits and vegetables, or foods prepared on site such as an international food court. Finally, a Mercado, even on a small-scale, provides a multitude of small business and entrepreneurial opportunities for members of the Oak View community.

The community center element of Concept A is a smaller, supplemental facility to what is already located in Oak View. We envision meeting rooms, teen sturdy areas, a technology center, and maybe even offices for a micro-enterprise incubator that could fund the small businesses Concept A would generate. The Community Center would be a valuable asset to Oak View and would provide a myriad of social, economic, and physical programs and amenities for neighborhood residents.

A final amenity in the Concept A design is a community garden. The items grown at this site could be later sold through the Mercado, or a small-scale food manufacturing site can be established next to the garden where the community could start a micro-enterprise and create condiments, sauces etc. for sale locally. Community gardens have also proven to be great community spaces to provide educational opportunities for kids to learn about agriculture and nature, and also as a gathering place for events as varied as a health fair or voter registration sign-up.

Concept B

In Concept B, the focus shifts to the community center and park/open space elements. In this design, we envision an almost complete replacement of existing facilities with a 25,000 sq. ft community center. This vision includes an expanded library, children's reading room, separate study areas for teens and pre-teens, a technology center, and meeting rooms for residents.

There would also be income generating opportunities, specifically through renting spaces for: a post office sub station that would offer a local post office for mailing and money order purchase, a utility kiosk for residents to pay bills, meeting rooms for surrounding businesses, and offices for local non-profits. A weekend farmers market held in the community center parking lot could serve as another revenue generator in the community.

The park, recreational and open space design elements include a community garden as well as basketball courts, a tot lot next to the community center, and a soccer field with flexible design. It could be one large field or several children's fields. Soccer fields and field space in general are valuable commodities in southern California and can be strictly community-focused or rented out to outside agencies as an income generating strategy.

flexible design. It could be one large field or several children's fields. Soccer fields and field space in general are valuable commodities in Southern California and can be strictly community-focused or rented out to outside agencies as an income generating strategy.

Concept C

The third alternative is a more traditional mixed use, retail and office development that includes a small community center as a supplement to existing facilities. The office and retail part of this design, through new market tax credits, could generate income for the community, similar to Market Creek in San Diego. The tax income generated would stay in the Oak View community to be used for a variety of infrastructure and Community needs. The retail/office element of this design could also include spaces for micro-enterprise businesses, as well as a business incubator for funding and business ownership training. The Park element is a community garden by the community center with the parking screened from existing residence.

The Gateway Redevelopment Plan provides three design alternatives for an under-utilized parcel in the heart of the Oak View community. It is our hope that these design alternatives inspire hope and motivation for the Oak View partnership, and the Oak View community, to realize the full social and economic benefits of this parcel. Oak View is a community that would greatly benefit from any combination of these design alternatives, and our hope is that this parcel can become a landmark, visionary development that addresses the current and future needs of Oak View.

SUMMARY

Implementation Guidelines

Introduction

The purpose of this section in the report is to provide the framework for implementing the ideas and findings presented by the two design groups and the community assessment group. The ideas presented in this chapter draw from a variety of traditional and non-traditional financial tools. The types of financial tools that can be used include, but are not limited to, Community Development Financial Institutions/New Market Tax Credits, Redevelopment Funds, Community Development Block Grants, Foundational Grants, and Corporate Sponsorships. In addition, there are numerous public and private partnership opportunities available to the Oak View Renewal Partnership that can contribute to achieving the goals established within the community. Types of partnerships that the Oak View Community Renewal Partnership could pursue are ongoing work with the University of California, Irvine Department of Planning, Policy and Design, and the Community Outreach Partnership Center. Each of these financial and partnership tools are discussed in greater detail below.

Self-Evaluation of the Board Capabilities

A central goal of this report has been to provide the Renewal Partnership with a plan for addressing some of the problems within the Oak View Community. A critical part of this process, however, is prioritizing the resources and skills that are available to the Partnership. In reviewing the implementation strategies presented here, the Board members should ask three questions:

1. Is the Board capable of doing this internally?

2. Does the Board need to partner with outside agencies or organizations to use this implementation strategy?

3. Does the Board need to contract with outside agencies or organizations to use this implementation strategy?

The answers to these questions will provide the Board with direction on where to place its efforts and limited resources. Some of the implementation strategies that are presented here, such as writing a grant, could be fulfilled by the Oak View Renewal Partnership. Other implementation strategies, such as using new market tax credits, wi11 almost certainly require the Board to contract with an outside agency for help securing and expending the tax credits. In the following sections, a more thorough discussion of each implementation strategy is conducted.

Community Development Financial Institutions (CDFIs)

Community Development Financial Institutions are development finance entities organized to serve defined communities that are underserved by conventional capital markets, such as low-income communities like Oak View. Various funding opportunities and structures exist under this designation, some more applicable to Oak

View than others. Funding for CDFIs often comes from community and religious organizations, private banks and investors, but the majority comes from the Community Development Financial Institutions Fund created by the Federal government. The Fund was created to assist economically disadvantaged communities and their residents in gaining access to finances, and to encourage economic revitalization. Private banking institutions, like Bank of America, provide funding for CDFIs through Program Related Investments.

The federal CDFI Fund Program provides loans, equity investments, and grants to local and regional CDFIs. All CDFIs compete for federal support based on their business plan, market analysis, and performance goals. To receive financial assistance, CDFIs must provide matching private and non-federal funds to obtain CDFI Fund Support. The Core/Intelinediary Program is the Fund's primary program. This program provides technical assistance grants and capital funds to CDFIs and their intermediaries. The Small and Emerging CDFI Assistance (SECA) Program provides these same financial programs to establishing CDFIs and small existing entities. But the New Market Tax Credit Program can benefit Oak View the most out of the three.

The Clearinghouse CDFI in Lake Forest, which serves Orange, Riverside, San Bernardino, San Diego, and Los Angeles counties, can act as the CDE for the Oak View Community to filter and disperse funds for revitalization. The Clearinghouse CDFI is a for-profit corporation that provides direct loans for community development projects, affordable housing, small businesses, and other qualified Community Reinvestment Act (CRA) activities. The Clearinghouse CDFI has a separate division solely focused towards New Market Tax Credit (NMTC) services. This division is called the Clearinghouse NMTC. Under the Clearinghouse CDFI's umbrella, the Clearinghouse NMTC offers equity investments and loan services to businesses that may qualify for benefits under the

NMTC Program. More specifically, the NMTC loans, offered by the Clearinghouse NMTC, are available for construction financing, permanent financing, pre-development, community development, business loans (for working capital, business expansion, and start-up funds). The Clearinghouse CDFI has provided assistance to various communities in Southern California, most recently Market Creek Plaza in San Diego.

There are several financial tools that could be used for various needs that the Oak View Renewal Partnership may encounter. These needs can relate to workforce development/training or economic revitalization programs which could focus on infrastructure. No matter what type of CDFI type chosen, the Oak View Community can benefit from increasing financial education. There are many programs available to address community financial literacy for both adults and children, some designed for both to learn together.

The following is a short list:

1. Freddie Mac – Credit Smart Espanol

2. California Society of Certified Public Accountants – Dollars and Sense Workshop

3. Washington Mutual

    a. WaMoola for L.I.F.E ^{TM} Lessons, Grades K-12

    b. Financial Education Grants - For adults

3. National Council for Economic Education - Financial Fitness for Life

Redevelopment Funds

Redevelopment agencies' funds aim to address community blight and economic distress. Blight can be defined in physical and economic terms. One of the main tools redevelopment uses is tax increment financing. Current property taxes collected are capped to the time a redevelopment area is designated. Future tax increases, called the tax increment, go to the redevelopment agency to finance infrastructure improvements, site acquisition, real estate development and rehabilitation projects and other activities that support the revitalization of the redevelopment project area. At least 20% of the tax increment must be set aside to support and assist in the development, improvement, and preservation of affordable housing for low-and moderate-income residents.

The picture above shows the area designed by the city of Huntington Beach as a redevelopment area. Currently, over $1 million remains in the city's tax increment set-aside for low/moderate –income housing. The following is a list of projects eligible to receive these monies as defined by the California Redevelopment Association:

1. Acquire real property or building sites

2. Improve real property or building sites with onsite improvements

    •   Fundamental component of new construction or substantially rehabilitate affordable housing

    •   Improvements directly benefit low or mod income residents and that units remain available at affordable costs for periods in accordance with H & S Code Section 33334.3(c) and (f) (2).

3. Donate real property to private or public persons or entities (for use as low and moderate income housing)

4. Finance insurance premiums pursuant to H & S Code Section 33136

- Insurance premiums during the construction or rehabilitation of properties

5. Construct (low or moderate income) buildings or structures

   - Improving or increasing the supply of housing for low and moderate income person

6. Acquire buildings or structures (to be used for low and moderate income housing)

7. Rehabilitate buildings or structures (for use as low and moderate income housing)

8. Provide subsidies to, or for the benefit of, very low income households defined by (H & S Code Section 50105), lower income households (Section 50079.5) or persons and families of low or moderate income (Section 50093), to allow households to obtain housing at affordable costs on the open market

9. Pay principal and interest on bonds, loans, advances, or other indebtedness, or pay financing or carrying charges

   - Agencies can raise funds for housing projects by borrowing money and using housing fund monies as security

10. Maintain the community's supply of mobile homes

11. Preserve the availability to lower income households of affordable housing units in housing developments which are assisted or subsidized by public entities and which are threatened with imminent conversion to market ideas

    - Can be deed restricted

Community Development Block Grant Program (CDBG)

The Community Development Block Grant Program (CDBG) is a yearly allocation of funds from the U.S. Department of Housing and Urban Development (HUD). The CDBG program works to ensure decent affordable housing, to provide services to the most vulnerable in our communities, and to create jobs through the expansion and retention of businesses. The CDBG funds are designated to an entitlement area to be expended on programs designed to benefit persons of low and moderate income, prevent or eliminate blight, and address community development needs that are urgent but for which other funding is not available.

According to reports by the Department of Housing and Urban Development, during the FFY 2004/2005 Huntington Beach spent its CDBG allocations on youth and senior services, public facilities and parks and recreation (the report can be found at http://www. hud.gov/offices/cpd/communitydevelopment/library/accomplishments/ca/04 HuntingtonBeachC a.xls). The report indicates that over 42,000 people were benefited by the CDBG that was expended by the City. Huntington Beach's CDBG 2005/06 fund expenditure is $1.6 million and CDBG program expenditures for 2005/06 have been finalized by the City Council.

Process: The Citizen Participation Advisory Board (CPAB) holds public hearings on community need each year. CPAB members view presentations by applicants and may conduct site visits with participating agencies. The CPAB recommendations for CDBG funding are then forwarded to City Council for a public hearing and City Council approval.

Eligibility: Oak View community is eligible for CDBG activities because Oak View is one of eight Enhancement Areas. (CDBG requires that 70% of funds expended must benefit persons of 80% median income or less). Listed below are the types of activities that are eligible CDBG expenses and activities which are not eligible CDBG expenses (HUD 2006).

Eligible Activities

CDBG funds may be used for activities which include, but are not limited to:

- acquisition of real property;

- relocation and demolition;

- rehabilitation of residential and non-residential structures;

- construction of public facilities and improvements, such as water and sewer facilities, streets, neighborhood centers, and conversion of school buildings for eligible purposes;

- public services, within certain limits;

- activities relating to energy conservation and renewable energy resources; and

- provision of assistance to profit-motivated businesses to carry out economic development and job creation/retention activities.

Ineligible Activities

Generally, the following types of activities are ineligible:

- acquisition, construction, or reconstruction of buildings for government;

- political activities;

- certain income payments; and

- construction of new housing by units of general local government.

Foundational Grants

Foundations are a rich opportunity to obtain funding for Oak View Partnership, Mathes Uthdm other affiliated groups. It is important to write grant proposals that match the vision of the foundation. A list of potential fenders is provided in Appendix D of this report. These have been selected based on the foundations' areas of interest. Other resources for choosing a foundation include:

- Orange County Volunteer Center (www.volunteercenter.org)

- The Foundation Center (www.fdncenter.org)

Oak View Partnership may apply for grants that focus on programs the following program areas:

- Community Development - Homeownership

- Economic vitality - Workforce Development - Job Training - Financial literacy

- Sustainable communities

- Grassroots organizing

- Government/civic participation

- Minority/immigrant services - Race relations - Historically underserved

- Low-income services

- Youth services - After school programs - Encouraging secondary education

- Women

- Health/ Wellness

- Technology

A good rule of thumb for writing grants is to think <u>SMART:</u> <u>S</u>pecific, <u>M</u>easurable, <u>A</u>chievable, <u>R</u>ealistic, <u>T</u>ime bound. Grant proposals should identify a specific program, outline measurable outcomes, provide a plan for implementation, state how the applicant will evaluate the success of a program, and how the program will be sustained after the foundation grants money (i.e. other sources of funding, sponsorships, available resources and staff support). Proposals should also include a brief background on the community that will be served.

Most foundations do not like to fund Orange County because if its reputation of wealth and affluence. Grant proposals should dispel these myths and establish a critical need for funding in Huntington Beach. The following are good sources of demographic information to include in grant proposals:

- Orange County Community Indicators Report - Includes information on race, poverty, housing affordability, home-lessness, health and more: <u>http://www.oc.ca.gov/ceo-community.asp</u>

- GIS Map Generator - Maps out demographics, housing and other statistics: <u>http://geography.Fullerton.edu/uwmap-ping/HuntingtonBeach/gismain.htm</u>

- U.S. Census Bureau American Fact Finder (research by Census tract): <u>http://www.census.gov</u>

Oak View Partnership may benefit from hiring a consultant to write grants, network with fenders, design programs, organize a budget and create plans for evaluation and sustainability. If unable to hire a professional consultant, Oak View Partnership can approach The University of California, Irvine Department of Planning, Policy and Design to request a student grant writer. This may be arranged through a grant writing course offered in the fall quarter (September - December)

Corporate Sponsorships

Corporate sponsorships are another viable option to provide funding and resources for Oak View. Local businesses may be solicited to sponsor anything from individual events, seasonal sports leagues or recreational facilities. Rainbow Disposal is an ideal corporate sponsor due to its location and employment of Oak View residents. Other potential sponsors include Starbucks Coffee, local banks and other nearby businesses. Many company websites include a link to information on sponsorships. It is also effective to phone a company and ask for their sponsorship or community relations representative. The process for applying for sponsorship is similar to grants, and most require submitting a proposal that outlines the event or program to be funded.

Potential Partners for the Oak View Community

All successful business endeavors require a stable and refined plan from the head institution and the enlistment of partners for support. The Oak View community can stand to benefit and promote long-term success with the right combination of financial and community involvement. Partnerships made with businesses, academic institutions, local governments and political personalities can only strengthen the vision for this community. The information below is brief introduction to the potential partners the community of Oak View could stand to benefit from if involved in a working relationship.

Property Owners

The property owners are the first major advocates the Renewal Partnership needs to get support from. This may be difficult, as almost all property owners live outside the community, city and a few outside of the state. It would be beneficial to outline your goals for them and have them understand what is expected and encouraged from them by providing them with a list involvement ideas and resources. For major structural and capital improvements to properties, there are city-sponsored loans and grant programs available at low interest rates. Property owners are a foundational partnership for the Oak View Renewal Project and critical to the future of the community.

Clearinghouse CDFI

This could be the economic funding engine that Oak View needs to jumpstart its improvement process. Their mission is to provide neighborhoods from all income and ethnic backgrounds with access to credit for improvement opportunities. In 2004 alone they have loaned over \$31 million to California communities. They specialize in loans for Community Development and Affordable Housing, two important topics for Oak View. As mentioned above, New Market Tax Credits provide an innovative financing mechanism for securing funds for all kinds of projects. The Clearing House also has a division called Affordable Housing Clearing House, specializing in helping families purchase their first homes in addition to supplying credit information, finance and loan education.

The City of Huntington Beach

The City of Huntington Beach needs to be involved at some point during the Oak View renewal process because to get any kind of improvement project done in the city, the board will eventually have to have their plans approved by the Planning Commission and City

Council. Putting past opinions and experiences aside, the City can be a big supporter by sponsoring events on holidays, neighborhood clean-ups and acting as a guiding council to make sure some of the long term goals of the Oak View Community are consistent with the rest of the city. Ideally, the City will see the potential in Oak View and the motivation and dedication of the residents and board and be moved to take a more active role.

University of California, Irvine
UC Irvine is one of the top rated research universities in the University of California school system. UCI is home to the department of Planning, Policy and Design (PP&D), which strives to involve graduate students in research opportunities in and around Orange County. The PP&D department houses the Community Outreach Partnership Center (COPC), which looks to build bridges between UCI and the local community by engaging UCI faculty and students. COPC supports research, teaching, and outreach projects that focus on demographic change and its impacts for communities. Also within the PP&D department is the Center for Community Health Research (CCHR) which focuses on the advancement of the science of community health through interdisciplinary research involving local stakeholders in planning for their own health. These would be great tools for funding, research and involvement for the Oak View Renewal project.

Local Businesses
Whether they are small retail, office or commercial entities, local businesses have a right to know the changes taking place in their neighborhood. They could affect profits and possible relocation depending on the project's implementation. Local businesses are good sources of advertisement and sponsorship for local events on holidays or special events. Many might be willing to offer

promotions or contests through the schools or be willing to make donations for certain community projects.

Local, County and State Representatives
As important as gathering local resident, owner and business support for the Oak View Renewal Project is, recognition in the political arena will give this community much deserved promotion. From council members, district representatives and up through the county and state seats, Oak View needs to put their changes on the radar of those involved in politics. Attention and funding are all possible if endorsed by the right elected official. Politicians often look for communities who decide to change and in an effort to support them and their own political agenda, will publicly speak on behalf of a community like Oak View.

This is just a brief introduction to number of different partnerships the community of Oak View should consider bringing on board when they move forward with their plan. The three key elements recognized in all successful projects are forming great partnerships, proper and timely execution of the plan and the support and help of great people. Oak View has the makings for all three.

Conclusion
Implementation of the strategies provided in this report requires a close evaluation of Oak View Renewal Partnership's ability to manage programs, apply for funding and foster relationships with outside entities. Consultants and partnerships may be utilized to expand the Board's capacity. A Directory of Resources is provided in Appendix D, listing contact information to initiate a range of activities. See Appendices B-H for further resources including implementation outlines, spreadsheets and directories.

Appendix A
Oak View Questionnaire

Cuestionario de Oak View

Participant(s):_____
(Participantes):

Neighborhood Conditions (Condiciones de l a vecinclad):

1. Living Conditions (i.e. environment, streets, parks, open space, playground, sidewalk) Condiciones de vida (ambiente, calles, parques, areas abiertas, areas de juego, aceras)

2. Housing Conditions (Physical Structures - interior and exterior) Condiciones de las vivienda (estructura fisica - interior e exterior)

3. Would resident(s) like to improve their housing/living conditions through rehabilitation? If so, what would they like to improve?

Quisieran los residentes mejorar sus condiciones de villa/vivienda mediante rehabilitation? En caso de ser correcto, que aspectos quisieran mejorar?

4. Do resident(s) feel that the Oak View Community needs new housing units?
   Sienten los residentes que el Oak View Community necesita unidades de vivienda nuevas?

5. How do resident(s) feel about their rent level, too high, ok, just right, etc?
   Como se sienten 1os residentes acerca del nivel del alquiler? Muy alto, más o menos, tal como debe ser, etc?

6. Would residents consider homeownership if possible?
   De ser posible, considerarian los residentes ser propietarios de su propia vivienda?

7. How many people live in one unit (apartment or house)?
   How long have resident(s) live in Oak View?
   Cuantas personas viven en una unidad (apartamento o casa)
   Cuanto tiempo llevan los residentes en Oak View?

8. Other concerns (i.e. rat problem)
   Otras preocupaciones (ej. problema con ratas)

Safety Concerns

9. Do resident(s) feel safe in their neighborhood (i.e. walking around)?
   Se sienten los residentes seguros en su vecindario (ej. saliendo a caminar)?

10. What area(s) do resident(s) feel safe in?
    En clue areas se sienten los residentes seguros?

11. What area(s) do resident(s) feel unsafe in?
En cjue areas se sienten los residentes inseguros?

12. How do resident(s) feel about the street lights (i.e. enough lighting)?
Como se sienten los residentes acerca del alumbramiento de las calles (e j. existe suficiente luz)?

13. Is there sufficient police force?
Existe suficiente fuerza policial?

14. Other concerns (i.e. crimes, violence)
Otras preocupaciones (e j. crimenes, violencia)

15. Do resident(s) have concerns with the traffic flow within the community (i.e. cars traveling too fast - need barriers)?
Tienen los residentes preocupaciones en cuanto al nivel de trafico en la comunidad (ej. carros que viajan demasiado rápido -se ocupa algun tipo de barreras)?

Accessibility

16. Are they able to access places they need to go via public buses?
Existen formas de accesar los lugares que frecuentan, mediante buses publicos?

17. Would they consider the Car-share program?
Considerarian programas en los cuales se comparten automobiles?

18. Other concerns
Otras preocupaciones

Economic Feasibility

19. What type of stores/shops/restaurants would resident(s) like to have nearby (i.e. Hispanic market farmer's market)? Que tipo de mercados/tiendas/restaruantes le gustaria a los residentes tener cerca (ej. mercado latino, mercado de granjeros)?

20. Would resident(s) like to have a community owned OR their own stores/shops/restaurants? If so, what type of business? Les gustaria a los residentes tener mercados/tiendas/restaurants poséidos por ellos mismos o por la comunidad? *Si este es el caso, que tipo* de *negocio?*

Amenities

21. What are the existing amenities (i.e. shopping, entertainment, laundry, recreation, sports)? Cuales son las amenidades existents (ej. tiendas de compras, entretenimiento, lavenderias, recreation, deportes)?

22. Are the existing amenities sufficient? Son suficientes las amenidades actuales?

23. Do resident(s) commute (near or far) outside Oak View in search of particular amenity(ies)? Tienen los residentes que viajar (cerca o lejos) fuera de Oak View en busca de ciertas amenidades?

Ideas for the Vacant Lot (owned by Rainbow Disposal)
(Ideas para el terreno vacio (adueñaclo por Rainbow Disposal)

1. Community gardens?
   Jardines comunitarios?

2. Frarmer's market?
   Mercados de granjeros?

3. Community Center? (What should be included?)
   Centro de Comunidad?

   Vision for the Community
   Vision ram la comunidadl

   Additional Comments
   Comentarios adicionales

Appendix B
Implementation Outline Based on UCI Recommendations

(Some overlap in ideas exist)

<u>Direct Outside Support</u>

- CDFI - Clearinghouse CDFI

- Professional Grant Writer

- Sponsorships

- Street lighting consultant

- WIFI Company

<u>Things on the Board's "To Do List"</u>

- Evaluate:

  1. Board Capabilities

  2. Volunteers

  3. Support Staff

- Identify:

  1. Banking experience of Board members

  2. Implementation Team

  3. Grant Writers

- Relationships:

  1. City of Huntington Beach

  2. Orange County Housing Authority, Children & Families Commission, etc.

  3. Assemblyman Harmon

  4. Local Businesses - Fundraising opportunities

  5. Americorps

- Prepare financial statement and budget

- Outline steps necessary to meet goals:

  1. Primary, Intermediary, etc.

  2. Short-term, Long-term, etc.

Partners outside the Oak View Renewal
Partnership

Short-term (ST) - next year, Long-term (LT) - beyond the next year

- UCI:

  1. Grantwriting Class (ST, LT)

  2. Professional Report/Research Opportunity (ST)

      3. COPC - Community Outreach Partnership Center (LT)

      4. UCI Volunteer Center - Potential Opportunity (ST)

      5. Social Ecology Internship Course - Potential Opportunity (ST)

- City of Huntington Beach Departments

      1. Assemblyman Harmon (ST, LT)

      2. Redevelopment Agency (ST, LT)

      3. Parks & Recreation (ST, LT)

      4. Code Enforcement (ST, LT)

      5. School Districts (ST, LT)

      6. Police Department (ST, LT)

- Americorps (ST, LT)

- For-Profit CDE funding recipients (ST, LT)

- Day labor center (ST, LT)

- Dental/Medical Health Services - Possibly UCI Students (ST, LT)

- Orange County Human Relations Council - Community Watch (ST, L

Appendix C
Opportunities based on UCI Recommendations

(Some overlap in ideas exist)

Education/Social Services

- Children and Young adult programs Ages 10 and older
    1. Middle and High-school students, and adults
    2. Literacy
        a. Financial Education (CDFI, Washington Mutual, Wells Fargo)
        b. English & Spanish language classes
- Wireless Community
- Computer Classes
- Job Training
- Health Clinics/Wellness Center (Nutritional & General Health Education)
- Dental Services/Education
- Summer College Scholarships & Camps
- Neighborhood Pride Programs

<u>Technology</u>
- Computer Facility
- WIFI Connection
- **ROP – Trade skills**

Financial
- Education
- CDBG – Rehabilitation
- NMTC (must have revenue source)
  1. Community Center
  2. Mixed-Use
- Sponsorships
  1. Verizon
  2. Recreation Programs
- Grants
  1. Education
  2. Business & Community
  3. Housing
  4. Medical/Dental/Wellness
- CDFI Loans
  1. Community Center (Non-revenue source)
  2. Trash Enclosures

Appendix D
Directory Of Resources

JOB ASSISTANCE
City of Huntington Beach Business Development

714-536-5582

http://www.surfcity-hb.org/CityDepartments/ED/BusinessDevelopment

Job Center, Financial Assistance, Business Site Location, Local Resources

Luis M. Ochoa Job Center

(714) 841-0637

http://www.ci.huntingtonbeach.ca.us/CityDepartments/ED/BusinessDevelopment/jobcenter.cfui .

Open all 7 days per week, 6am till noon

18131 Gothard Street (South of Talbert)

Huntington Beach, CA 92647

HOUSING ASSISTANCE
City of Huntington Beach Housing Department

714-536-5582

http://www.ci.huntington-beach.ca.us/CityDepartment/ED/Housing/

Rental Assistance, Ownership Programs

Orange County Housing & Community Services

714-480-2900

http://www.ochousing.org/

Rental Assistance, Housing Loans and Financing, Workforce Services, Human Relations

STREET IMPROVEMENTS

City Services/Public Works

Field Service Representative 714-375-5010 Monday through Friday, 7 a.m. to 4 p.m. http://www.surfcity-hb.org/Residents/city services/

Animal Control, Street Sweeping, Civil Citation Payments, Traffic Signals & Street Lights, Graffiti Removal, Utility Services, Library Services, Waste Disposal Information, Parking Ticket Payment Information, Passport Services

General Number 714-536-5431

http://www.surfcity-hb.org/CityDepartments/Public_Works/

COMMUNITY SERVICES

City of Huntington Beach Community Services

714-536-5486

http://www.surfcity-hb.org/CityDepartments/Comm Services/

Sports Facilities, Community Centers, Rental Facilities, Meeting Spaces, Cultural Services

Huntington Beach Libraries

714-842-4481

http://www. surfcity-hb.org/CityDepartments/Library/

Huntington Beach School District

714-964-8888

http://www.hbcsd.k12.ca.us/

Huntington Beach Police Department

714-960-8811

http://www.hbpd.org/

GOVERNMENT REPRESENTATIVES

City of Huntington Beach

http://www.ci.huntington-beach.ca.us/

City Council

714-536-5553

Political Concerns, Relationship with City, Availability of Resources

California State Legislators

Assembly District 67

Assemblyman Tom Harmon

Capitol Phone: 916-319-2067

Huntington Beach Phone: 714-843-4966 http://republican.asembly.ca.gov/members/index.asp?Dist=67&lang=1

Senate District 35 Vacant

FUNDING SOURCES (Not Foundations)

City of Huntington Beach Redevelopment Agency

714-536-5582

http://www. surfcity-hb. org/CityDepartments/ED/redevelopment/

Funding Contact: Steve Holtz

Federal and State Funding (Community Development Block Grant, Tax-Increment Financing Funds), General Needs for Economic and Community Vitality

Clearinghouse CDFI

949-859-3600

http://sites.wsupdate.com/cdfi/

New Markets Tax Credit

Rainbow Disposal

714-817-3581

http://www.rainbowdisposal.com/

Other Potential Sponsors

Local Businesses

Local B anks

Local WIFI-Technological Companies (i.e. Verizon, SBC, AT&T, Dell)

For-profit Community Development Entity funding recipients

GRANT WRITERS & PROGRAM CONSULTANTS

UC Irvine Grant Writing Course

Anne O1in, Lecturer

949-679-7093

www.theolingroup.com

Provides student to provide free grant writing service for September - December

Urban Land Institute Advisory Services

Provides technical expertise of ULI members to cities, private developers, and other organizations that need objective analysis and advice on how to solve a difficult land use, development, and redevelopment problems

http://www.uli.org/Content/NavigtionMenu/ProgramsServices/AdvisoryServices/AdvisoryServices.htm

Urban Land Institute District Council Technical Assistance Programs (TAPS) Conducted by local ULI members, TAPs are a 1-day session in which a local government or non-profit organization asks the District Council to provide advice on a specific land use issue.

http://www.uli.org/Content/NavigationMenu/ ProgramsServices/AdvisoryServices/Option/Optioins.htm

UNIVERSITY PARTNERSHIPS – RESEARCH & SERVICES

UC Irvine Department of Planning Policy & Design

Graduate Student Professional Report

Kristen Day

949-824-5880

UC Irvine Community Outreach Partnership Center

Victor Becerra, Director

949-824-9337

VOLUNTEER PROGRAMS

UC Irvine Volunteer Center

Edgar Dormitorio, Director

949-824-8045

Office of Service Learning, Chapman University http://www.chapman.edu/lead/service/default.asp

Jessica Eddings

Service Learning Coordinator

714-997-6908

eddin100@chapman.edu

Brittany Zemlick

Service Learning Coordinator 714-997-6908

zemli100@champman.edu

Volunteer & Service Center, CSU Fullerton 714-278-7623

http://www.fullerton.edu/deanofstudents/volunteer/

AmeriCorps

http://www.americorps.org/for_organizations_how/index.asp

OTHER POTENTIAL RESOURCES

Dental/Medical Health Services -UCI Medical Students

Local Universities/Colleges for Summer College and Minority Recruitment Programs Orange County Human Relations Council

Property Owners

Developers

Appendix E: OakView Collaborative

Steering Committee Partners

Fact Funded Partners

Karen Catabijan, O.V.S.D. Oak View Elementary School 17241 Oak Lane Huntington Beach, CA 92647 (714) 842-4459 FAX #: (714) 842-4769 kcatabijan@ovsd.org	Linh LY Interval House P.O.Box 3356 Seal Beach, CA 90740-2356 (562) 594-9492 ext 205 FAX #: (562) 596-3370 admin@intervalhouse.org
Sherri Medrano Oak View Elementary School 17241 Oak Lane Huntington. Beach, CA 92647 (714) 847-1456 FAX #: (714) 842-4587 smedrano@ovsd.org	Nanci Williams Huntington Beach Central Library 7111 Talbert Ave Huntington Beach, CA 92648 (714) 374-5106 FAX #: (714) 3741616 williamn@surfcity-hb.org

Elsa Greenfield
CSP, Inc.
1821 East Dryer Rd. - Suite 200
Santa Ana, CA 92705
(949) 250-0488
FAX #: (949) 251-1659
egreenfield@csplnc.org
	Mary Pat Gonzalez
	Huntington Beach Central
	  Library
	7111 Talbert Ave
	Huntington Beach, CA 92648
	  (714) 374-5107 or (714)
	  374-5332
	  (714) 374-1616
	gonzalesm@surfchb.org

Sharon Wie Interval House P.O.Box 3356 Seal Beach, CA 90740-2356 (562) 594-9492 FAX #: (562) 596-3370 saron@ih.org	Janet Judson Huntington Beach Central Library 7111 Talbert Ave Huntington Beach, CA 92648 (714) 375-5106 FAX #: (714) 374-1616 judsoni@surfcity-hb.org
Janine Limas Interval House P.O.Box 3356 Seal Beach, CA 90740-2356 (562) 594-9492 FAX #: (562) 596-3370 adman@intervalhouse.org	Claudia Locke Oak View Branch Library 17241 Oak Lane Huntington Beach. CA 92647 (714) 375-5068 Fax#: (714) 375-5073 lockec@surfcity-hb.org

Michelle Pellicino, Program Coordinator Camp Fire USA 14742 Plaza Dr., Suite 205 Tustin, CA 92780 (714) 838-9991 FAX: (714) 838-0567 info@ campfireusaoc.org	Barbara Ten Broek Children's Bureau 50 S. Anaheim blvd., Suite 241 Anaheim, CA 92805 (714) 517-1900 x218 Cell: (714) 863-0873 FAX: (714) 517-1911 btenbroek@all4kids.org
Lisa Arcand, LCSW Western Youth Services 10101 Slater Ave. - Suite 241 Fountain Valley, CA 92708 (714) 378-2620 FAX: (714) 378-2631 larcand@ westernyouthservices.org	TECHNICAL SUPPORT YMCA (CDBG FUNDED) Gavin Reath 2100 Main Street Huntington Beach, CA 92648 (714) 847-9622 x109 FAX: (714) 969-4080 greath@ymca.oc.net website: www.ymcaoc.org
Lorry Leigh, ED Western Youth Services Administrative Office 10101 Slater Ave. - Suite 241 Fountain Valley, CA 92708 (949) 855-1556 FAX: (714) 378-2631 lleigh@westernyouthservices. org	

OAK VIEW COLLABORATIVE

STEERING COMMITTEE PARTNERS
Non-Funded Partners

Carol Kanode Ocean View High School 17071 Gothard St. Huntington Beach, CA 92647 (714) 848-0656 x 429 FAX #: (714) 842-9846 carolkanode@yahoo.com	Marlene Kline Huntington Beach Union High School District/Adult School 16666 Tunstall Ave. Huntington Beach, CA 92647 (714) 847-2873 x 214 FAX #: (714) 841-2283 mkline@hbsdultschool.com

Marti Whitford
Community Health Centers
8041 Newman Ave.
Huntington Beach, CA 92647
(714) 847-4222 x 220
FAX #: (714) 842-4359
mwhitford@hbclinic.org
	Amy Blanford
	Oak View Child Development
	   Center
	17341 Jacqueline Lane
	Huntington Beach, CA 92647
	(714) 842-4064
	FAX #: (714) 842-5814 aybd@
	   aol.com

Sandra Vega Community Health Centers 8041 Newman Ave. Huntington Beach, CA 92647 (714) 847-4222 x 406 FAX: (714) 843-0676 sguerra@hbclinic.org	Jack Shaw El Viento P.O.Box 3897 Huntington Beach, CA 92605 (714) 813-6593 FAX 895-8222 johncshaw@earthlink.net

Alejandro Tovares Community Health Centers 8041 Newman Ave. Huntington Beach, CA92647 (714) 847-4222 FAX: (714)842-9843 amtovares@tnsn.com	Zayda Garcia El Viento P.O.Box 3897 Huntington Beach, CA 92605 (714) 892-7711 ext 55236 FAX 895-8222 zaarcia@elvlento.org
Pat Sterling RN, PHN Health Care Agency 14180 Beach Blvd. Santa Ana, CA 92702 (714) 896-7804 FAX #: (714) 896-7808 psteriing@ochca.com	Josefina Bay, Promotora Latino Health Access 1717 N. Broadway Santa Ana, CA 92705-2605 (714) 542-7792 ext 3155 FAX: (714) 647-2645 www. LatinoHealthAccess.org
Donna Brush, Even Start Coordinator Oak View Preschool 17131 Emerald lane Huntington Beach, CA 92647 (714) 843-6938 FAX: (714) 375-6354 dbrush@ovsd.org	Alex Vasquez, Promoter Latino Health Access 1717 N. Broadway Santa Ana, CA 92705-2605 (714) 542-7792 ext 3154 FAX: (714) 647-2645 www.LatinoHealthAccess.org
Joyce Horowitz, Director Oak View Preschool 17131 Emerald Lane Huntington Beach, CA 92647 (714) 843-6938, ext. 2873 FAX: (714) 375-6354 jhorowitz@ovsd.org	Linda Franco, Project Director Volunteers of America 17479 Beach Boulevard Huntington Beach, CA 92647 (714) 842-7476 FAX: (714) 847-3845 talentsearchhb@verizon.net

Kathleen Yutchishen Oak View FRC Health Access Program 17261 Oak Lane Huntington Beach, CA (714) 596-7072 FAX: (714) 842-5796 kathleenyutchishen@ all4klds.org	Community United Methodist Church Joan Armstrong 6652 Hell Ave Huntington Beach, CA 92647 (714) 842- 4461

51378474R00146

Made in the USA
Middletown, DE
02 July 2019